The Playbacks of Jim Klobuchar

The Playbacks
of
Jim Klobuchar

by Jim Klobuchar

A mixed harvest from society's
playfields and battlefields
by the **widely-read** columnist
of The Minneapolis Star.

DILLON PRESS
Minneapolis, Minnesota 55401

Library of Congress Number 75-96867
Copyright 1967 by the
Minneapolis Star and Tribune Co.
Published by Dillon Press, Inc.
Minneapolis, Minnesota U.S.A.

This book is for my
charitable family and
my forgiving editors

Table of Contents

Foreword

Because of the speedy mortality of the day's newspaper, the conventional fate of its merchandise is a dignified oblivion whereby it is filed, melted or given some similar enshrinement.

Usually this is by common consent of (a) the readers (b) the publishers and (c) the authors, and sometimes at the urging of one or the other. This is to say a decent burial at the end of the day may not be deserved but demanded.

Occasionally some of it is exhumed, however, to be granted the less dignified fate of republication. This is in response to no special pleading by any of the parties but simply because the practice has acquired respectability over the years, from repetition if nothing else.

As an excuse for burdening readers with part of his work for a second time, the author admits this is somewhat underpowering in its urgency. Your tolerance and charity, therefore, will have to extricate him from the vulnerable defensive posture in which he has dangled himself.

This is the second small volume of its type since I began writing a column for the Minneapolis Star in 1965. The first achieved some local celebrity as not necessarily the best book of the year but certainly one of the thinnest.

We may only guess at what comparable niche of novelty this one may aspire to.

Whatever value the original work might have in the way of diverting, informing or persuading has been diluted, I know, by time. If there is any real justification for it, though, it is this: The human spirit occasionally yens for a reflective backward look, when it may recapture an event, an emotion or some little delirium.

If the presidential campaign of 1968, for example, is beginning to fog in memory, there is material here that may transport the reader back into the dinning convention halls; or for the baseball fan, back into Billy Martin's private armory; or for the science-fiction buff, back into the California rain forests wherein is supposed to dwell the hairiest creature of them all.

The material is drawn both from the writer's columns in The Star and from news-feature dispatches that appeared in the publication's news pages. Some of the latter flows from field assignments in which the editor and author maintained an even balance of puzzlement. The author was puzzled by the originality of the assignment and the editor was equally mystified by the originality of the author's expense account.

I am indebted once more to the publishers of The Star, the John Cowles family, for their cooperativeness in making the material available and, over the years, for their sense of trust and fondness of suspense.

There is material here which, now and then, tries to perform some stitchwork on the public figures of the territory and the institutions. Without blushing for it, I would like to note that virtually all of it is done in the spirit of good-tempered jousting in which the author sought to leave enough of his flank showing to invite an atoning dart.

What could be more convivial?

Jim Klobuchar, September, 1969

The Universe Held Its Breath

They moved under the glass of eternity, their every movement and word a triumph of the ages. But they were Tom Sawyer and Huck Finn more than they were Columbus and Magellan, and there was more unquenchable humanity in their impulsive chatter than in the marvel of their deed.

A quarter of a million miles from earth, on the sun-bleached desert of another world, Buzz Aldrin peered at the little hump of rubble in front of him and announced with a bright sense of discovery:

"Neil, I told you we'd find some purple rocks."

Armstrong sounded impressed, as he might have thirty years ago when a slough-prowling buddy had just disclosed the presence of the largest bullfrog in the pond.

We were closer to them, I think, than we imagined in that unbelievable two hours when we were numbed not only by the immensity of their act but by the ease with which we were made witness to it.

It is no rhetoric exercise to say we all walked on the moon with them. We did so partly because it was history's most majestic journey of the human spirit which we all yearned to share, but mostly because the two who were there made the moon a playground as much as a laboratory.

Oh, they were astronauts and scientists and test pilots, all right, but we understood them best when they bounced around on the surface like 12-year-old kids in the first snow.

This might explain why their off-the-cuff dialogue and their delighted discoveries captivated us, where the language and the stunts intended for history are quickly forgettable.

Thus, Captain Neil leaves the module and with his first stride onto the soil of the moon declares, "One small step for a man, one giant leap for mankind." It has a well-honed style, but it didn't strike with the same blend of the fairy-tale and the sidewalk slang as "Houston, I'm on the porch."

The technological miracles of our time move with such stunning speed that it is difficult to grasp in two short hours of this visit to another planet how giddy it all really is.

Armstrong descends warily, dipping a tentative toe into the sand. The heroics out of the way, he jumps onto the moon and practically shouts to Aldrin: "Not a creature in sight."

Like the first photographer ever born, he forgets the time of day and starts shooting pictures despite the gentle prodding from his overseers on earth about contingency scoops of rocks and soil.

Somewhat apologetic, he scurries away from the LEM and tells Houston, "I think I'll try to get a rock over here." He has been on the moon only ten minutes, but he already is vaguely proprietary about it, the moon's first public relations man. "It's different," he reveals, "but it sure is pretty here."

And now Aldrin, emboldened by his pal's uneventful descent to the lunar landscape, comes bounding down the ladder and experiments with standing high jumps at the ladder's final rung.

They are together now, and we relax to enjoy the next two hours because we understand they are safe and we don't mind it that they will chide the scientists back at control with a few intramural needles about solar winds and core samples and level bubbles.

The scientists are in grim earnest about all of this and no doubt they should be, but science is outpointed by the fulfillment of our fantasies on the journey of Apollo, and this one is for the impish heart of man as much as it is for the test tube.

And so now they are frolicking around the module, experimenting with high knee action in the fashion of Hugh McElhenny running to daylight.

It was the ultimate sandlot for the spacesuit athletes from Outer Expressway, for the golfing duffer the biggest bunker in the solar system. At one-sixth gravity, Aldrin must be dying to try history's first 800-yard wedge shot.

There was a slow-motion, dream sequence quality to their flitting that gave it the appearance of a treasure hunt among the gnomes.

Houston observes all of this with good temper. "After you have finished with the solar winds and core samples," control tells them, "anything else you can put in the box will be acceptable."

They hustle about loading up a few more rocks which science tells us will unwrap the secrets of the universe.

"Get on up the ladder, Buzz," Houston says drolly.

He does, and Armstrong follows a few minutes later. Behind they leave a plaque inscribed: "We came in peace for mankind."

Does anyone doubt it?

The Roll Is Changed Up Yonder

The Roman Catholic church's surprising demotion of more than two hundred saints nervously reminds us once more that nobody is safe from the nosey files of the investigating committees.

Among the higher-ranking paragons who lost out in this most ecclesiastical squad cut in history were St. Christopher, the patron saint of travel, and St. Valentine, the spiritual protector of sweethearts through the ages.

The cashiering of St. Christopher, particularly, will shake millions of earthlings who attributed at least part of their good luck in avoiding parking lot dents to the intercession of this saintly traveler's aide, the spiritual forerunner of the friendly Standard Oil attendant.

The church's scholars now maintain there is serious doubt that Christopher, and forty-five other previously credentialed saints, ever existed. I admire its gallant pursuit of the truth in the face of pardonable snickers around the world, but there is an even more ominous message in this for the American car user. What it really means is that St. Christopher, having survived the ages of chariots, dugout canoes, oxcarts and streetcars, couldn't get past the 1969 model automobiles.

For those who haven't read the small print in the encyclicals, the Vatican Friday acted to de-clutter its calendar of feast days by dropping more than two hundred saints from the celestial honor roll.

It is hardly surprising that the Vatican's precipitate action set off some lively grousing in heaven. Do not ask me how this can be ascertained. If they can be reached by the Vatican's All Saints' enumerators, there is no reason why they can't be reached by telephone.

"It's really a blow," one of the de-canonized saints acknowledged in the small alcove where the second-ranking harpists are usually found. "After all these years, you figure you have enough seniority built up.

"It tells you all over again, there's just no such thing as sentiment any place in the world or, if you don't mind my saying it, even out of this world.

"The toughest news, though, was what happened to Christopher. We were talking about it just the other day. He was all set for a big year, what with the Maverick coming out and all. Well, you learn it every day, I suppose. You just can't take a thing for granted. Let me tell you, there are a lot of other guys around here sweating right now, and it would surprise you if I revealed their names."

"Even St. Nicholas, the pre-caloric Santa Claus, barely survived the cut and even he is now listed as optional. This means he is on waivers and may have to take another check-out ride, the final indignity."

He was reminded that while the situation might be embarrassing, it hardly compared with some of the more sweeping purges of recent times, such as the Legislature's overhaul of the university board of regents.

"For example," it was pointed out, "Valentine is off the liturgical calendar but still keeps his halo. Even the forty-six including Christopher still have an appeal coming and are eligible, in the words of the rites committee, 'to be venerated locally.'

"Yes, but it just isn't the same, is it?" he brooded. "What kind of status have you got being venerated locally. Nobody likes to be farmed out after all that time with the big club."

And yet, back on the ground, I encountered no exceptional bitterness among long-standing fans of the saints. Take Mr. Robert Provost, for instance, the Twin Cities insurance industry's interpreter, Provost is not only a driving expert but a Catholic. He is so safety-conscious, as a matter of fact, that whenever he goes into the confession booth he instinctively tells the cassocked priest to fasten his sash.

"Thousands of Catholics," he explained, "have been getting by as drivers by using—almost exclusively—the horn, brakes and St. Christopher statue. Catholic gift shops might compensate for their loss in the statuette-and-medal trade by teaching Catholics how to make graceless turns."

Mr. Adolph Block of the large Catholic church supply company of E. M. Lohmann in St. Paul seemed fretful. "It was bad enough when they dropped the missal, which was 30 percent of our business," he said. "I don't know what this latest thing will do, especially to our sterling silver Christopher models that go up to $20. It's sad to see so many of the saints going."

This is undoubtedly correct. I find one of own illusions crushed. The only time I ever won a track race for Ely was the day my Christopher medal flew off the neck chain, striking my nearest rival in the nose and dislodging him from his stride. I took it as providential, but it appears now it may have been a chuckhole in the track.

The hymn for the day, friends, is "When the Saints Go Marching Out."

Isaiah Could Have Called It

With a scriptural sense of destiny, the cast of characters materializes in the floodlit gloaming at Metropolitan Stadium. They come out of tunnels but it looks like the Apocalypse.

We are present at the most widely advertised morality play of the season, the meeting of our old plumed defender, the dragon-slaying Francis Tarkenton, and his one-time accomplices in purple, the Minnesota Vikings. Many of us here in the grandstand's Greek chorus are shot through with clashing emotions, while others of us are merely half shot.

Here he is in an alien blue helmet and a Giant uniform, St. Francis, the martyred millionaire, having just finished a five-minute macaroni commercial and therefore looking appropriately starchy.

On the other side of the benches is the protagonist coach, Bud Grant, who, of course, long since has been christened by morality play buffs as The Son of Gray Eagle. Bud stands motionless and impassive, canted slightly to the south, however, as though graven in a fixed position that enables him to set up for a field goal at any provocation.

Here on the field are the Four Horses from the Draft, who represent the Vikings harvest from the trade for Tarkenton. Their very names have a scriptural ring — Grim, Page, Washington and Jones. The latter may not be biblical, of course, but at least he is expensive.

You will recall another set of horsemen who emerged from revelations and discovered Notre Dame. These of the

Vikings, because they were high draft choices and costly, trace their origins not to Apocalypse but to Numbers.

Here in the press box is our good friend Sid Hartman, who is a kind of Moving Finger in this pageant. Sid is in the clutch of colliding passions, because he has been playing Isaiah all week and issuing black prophecies about the Viking future without Tarkenton. He is surrounded by clucking colleagues who want to know how Sid is going to vindicate his prophecy without rooting against the Vikings.

And, of course, from somewhere in the Louisiana canebrakes there is the voice of Norm Van Brocklin, having gone to his just reward as a television color announcer. He may be in New Orleans physically but this afternoon at the Met he is The Unseen Presence, hovering over us all and still wondering like the rest of us why in hell Francis handed off to Mayberry in the final two minutes with a field goal in the bank five years ago.

They are playing now, and on third and 12 on his own 10 in the first two minutes, Francis drops back. Now, I know Francis isn't going to pass. YOU know Francis isn't going to pass. Van Brocklin in New Orleans knows Francis isn't going to pass. But here comes big Carl Eller, trundling and thrashing with his outside rush and looking like the Specter of Doom. Eller DOESN'T know Francis isn't going to pass because the Vikings are innocents and never have played against a scrambling quarterback.

And so Francis gives big Carl the affectionate wave of one pal to another and runs slyly past him for a first down. Well, it is enough to pinch your heart seeing Francis do that to us, his old adoring public and stockholders, and the whole thing seems vaguely incestuous.

Francis spends the first 35 minutes happily throwing touchdown passes and this disturbs us because we want

to see the Vikings win, although it does not enrage us because Francis is a good man and an honored ex-ally. But
now Grim and Jones and Washington and Page begin to
exact retribution, aided by some fluttery-fingered New
York linebackers.

And quite suddenly the score is tied with a minute left
and here comes the final principal in the drama, the Shade
of Atonement, quarterback Joe Kapp. He shambles on
accompanied by an unmistakable clanking that may be
the sound of cast-off chains but in reality probably is a
loose case of Grain Belt.

Surrounded by all the glamour of Tarkenton, Grant,
Allie Sherman, and H. P. Skoglund's chauffeurs, Kapp is
the Nudnik of the ball game, having started badly and
not deviated significantly since then. But now the Vikings
stand at their own 35, and before Bud can set up for a field
goal Kapp is winding up. YOU know he is going to throw
to Washington. The announcers know he is going to throw
to Washington. And, in one of the heartening develop-
ments of the Viking offense, Washington knows he is going
to throw to Washington. But the Giants do not know, and
friends, we get Bud's field goal with 10 seconds left.

The moral is clear. We have seized the scepter from
Lombardi and, having now reached millenium, how about
making it two in a row?

The Rubdown Rosies of Lyndale Avenue

Briskly she kneaded my tired and deserving muscles, re-charging them, re-energizing them and in a few places, rearranging them.

"My good woman," I said, "you are stimulating but you are an imposter. This card advertising Lee's Sauna in Bloomington tells me you are a professional Oriental masseuse. Now you may be a professional and you may be a masseuse, but there is a suggestion of a North Sea spray in your eyes and a fjordish huskiness in your voice that tells me there is no way you can be an Oriental."

"That is correct," the young woman replied, rubbing my temple with a langorous circular movement. "I am a professional masseuse from Oslo. Do you want a refund?"

I weighed the alternatives and decided, with some reluctance which I'm sure you will understand, to continue my research. I had been asked by a couple of the more reputable social register battleaxes in Bloomington to investigate Lee's Sauna and confirm or deny the community gossip.

I'm not quite sure what the community gossip is supposed to be about, since it is difficult and frustrating to classify and subdivide all the gossip in Bloomington.

My verdict on Lee's Sauna: The place is legal, but just barely.

To arrive at this conclusion I had to undergo 45 minutes of suspenseful muscle therapy at the hands of a miniskirted blonde whose fingers may have lacked medical precision but at least had a certain exploratory resourcefulness.

"We manage," she explained, "to attract a pretty good clientele of sauna-lovers and thus stay out of debt."

"But how do you manage," I asked, "to stay out of jail?"

The elaborately-constructed blonde replied by spraying another dash of rubbing ointment on my shoulders and chiding me for my prudery in her murky Nordic tenor. There was an anesthetic fragrance of jasmine in the air, and faintly audible strings playing "Ebb Tide" nudged one's consciousness. I was falling asleep amid all of these zephyrs of fantasia that played about the room, and I was struck by the thought:

Every man in his own time must make harsh sacrifices such as this for the sake of his art and livelihood.

The blonde turned out to be not only a masseuse but a philosopher.

"We charge $9 for a sauna bath and massage. As you can see, everything is above board. We get men coming here who expect us to settle the problems of the universe for them in 45 minutes. The married ones are the worst. After a half-hour of my massaging, what do they expect, a psychoanalysis?"

"My dear young lady," I interrupted, "after a half-hour of your massaging it isn't a psychoanalysis they're looking for."

"Are you," she asked warily, "some kind of private detective?"

"All I am right now," I replied, "is overdone. Your sauna bath is erratic and seems vaguely tacked on to the whole operation. Do you get any trouble from the police?"

"Why? This is a perfectly respectable place, no matter what the housewives say. We get private detectives in here now and then and some plain clothesmen who are obviously from the Bloomington Police Department."

"Are they on duty?" I asked.

"I don't know whether they are on duty, but if they are, they certainly must be putting in overtime."

"How do you know they are plain clothesmen?"

"I used to work in a Cadillac agency in Boston. Most police characters drive Cadillacs, as you probably know. You get so you can spot police characters, whether they are in Boston or in Bloomington."

The masseuse glided aromatically around the rubbing table and kept asking me, "Are you absolutely sure you are comfortable?"

"Unfortunately," I said, "I have to make a telephone call to the city editor. I think he is beginning to worry."

"What," she said sadly, "a pity."

Delirium of the New Car Owner

A man experiences certain moments of soul-cleansing, emotional crisis—such as the purchase of a new automobile—when his heart convinces him the only thing that can mess up business in this country worse than the federal bureaucracy is private enterprise.

My car dealer is Hansord Pontiac, an agency which private gumshoes tell me is one of the better ones in the country. The maintenance shop is efficient and its rates are bearably high, a departure from some in town where the charges range from a standard minimum of exorbitant to a maximum of fraudulent.

Your normal delay while awaiting delivery of the car in Hansord's maintenance is what I would classify as endurable—meaning you can get by with two box lunches instead of three. This may cost you $20 or $30 in raw, inexcusable idle time, but they do serve free coffee.

And so one can live with these mildly offensive annoyances. It is the approaching disasters he has to be wary about.

I returned to Hansord a week or so ago because my last Pontiac was a mechanical prodigy. It rarely broke down and absorbed the customary parking lot bruises with forgiveness.

Confidentially, therefore, I confronted one of Hansord's higher megaton sales people, Don McDonald, who so far as I know is God-fearing, honest and successful—an extremely difficult parlay to achieve in the trade.

"McDonald," I said, "by dint of careful saving and by

extracting from the city editor an advance on the $3 a week he pays me for shoveling his walk, I am now moving up to air conditioning. I expect Hansord to sift out a veritable tangerine from the usual quota of first-run lemons, and I know I will live happily ever after in this car for the two years of its useful life."

McDonald immediately arrived at a sales figure and payment formula that persuaded me beyond doubt I was getting the best deal since Manhattan or at least since Southdale. In an aside to his mechanical people I overheard him saying, "This man is not only a car buyer but a newspaperman, the worst possible combination, and therefore must be considered potentially dangerous. At all costs his car should be flawless, in accordance with our standard and highest traditions."

A few days later I was summoned to the garage where McDonald dangled a key chain before me, tantalizing me with the prospect of indescribable automotive goodies and adventures ahead. "I will check you out immediately," he announced. The time was 3:45 p.m. The chronology:

3:47 p.m.—McDonald switches on the conditioning system and a blast of hot air bursts out of the coolant vents. "Just one of those small dislocations," he tuts. "There, the mechanic has switched the wires, and you are off."

9 p.m.—I emerge from a downtown parking lot, drive to the Cafe di Napoli, and park. The attendant asks if I would please move to another stall. I start to oblige. The engine will not turn over. The cafe manager scours the loop and finds a set of jumper cables. Power restored, I begin driving homeward, with a borrowed set of cables in the back seat as a precaution.

9:10 p.m.—I stop at an intersection, the engine stops and will not turn over. I connect the jumper cables to another battery, and the engine will not turn over. I summon AAA. "Did you say 18 miles on this automobile?" he asks. "Certainly," I respond, "what do you expect, perfection?" I am off again.

10:10 p.m.—I turn off the ignition in my driveway. Air is still blowing through the vents and will not stop. The battery gradually dies an agonized strangling death.

6 a.m.—I summon Town Taxi to come with the fourth set of jumper cables and I head toward the office. It is cool and I switch on the heater. I am impaled against the seat by a stream of polar air.

8:30 a.m.—The engine dies again outside the office and the men in the white frocks come to get my new automobile. The gauge reads 23 miles. I am out $18 in assorted costs and am wheel-less.

9:45 a.m.—McDonald calls. "A routine wiring problem," he says. "The car is now as good as new, which is appropriate since it is, well, almost new." I interrupt. "Why did you sell me that new set of four-ply tires, adding $155 to the bill," I ask. "The way you drive," he says, "you can't afford factory tires. Actually you're saving money."

McDonald has me convinced. And so it was with tolerance that I returned the car yesterday for a quick repacking of the door frame where wind was rushing in. But how in the hell am I going to drive to work without Steve Cannon? The radio is now out.

The Men and Their Cages

For the better part of a week, the writer shared the cell block, food and dialogue of the nearly 1,000 inmates of the Minnesota State Prison near Stillwater. His neighbor on one cell hall was a convicted murderer serving a life term, his partner on the kitchen serving line a rapist.

His conversation was a quiet struggle. He didn't want to whine, but he didn't want to accept being locked out forever from a society where he once prospered, and which now has exiled him as a murderer.

We sat beside each other, eating from our trays on a lacquered wood table top in the central dining hall of the Minnesota State Prison, where T. Eugene Thompson is serving a life term.

He was convicted more than four years ago of hiring men to murder his wife. He is still fighting the conviction, but his room for legal maneuver is narrowing.

He is cautious as we talk, but he tries to be responsive. I do not intend to try his case again, and he understands this. The khaki prison uniform and white undershirt give him the improbable appearance of an over-age Boy Scout. He looks neat, small and mild, his hair blonde and crew-cut.

"I try to get along," he says. "I'm still a clerk here. Full-time employment. The prison takes care of your needs, food, clothing, some leisure time recreation, so you really can't knock it very hard.

"You worry about getting institutionalized, though, because you want to hang onto your personality. I don't mean you try to be a nonconformist. It may serve the prison's needs to have a lot of faceless numbers here, but you fight that inside of yourself. I try, but if you're honest you find yourself blurring into some kind of formless existence.

"I suppose you can avoid that by rebelling, but that does you no good.

"I try to stay busy. It's bad to be introspective, to keep examining yourself. You find yourself looking back, at all of the good things that life outside the walls means.

"Some of the inmates here say you shouldn't look ahead, either. Serve one day at a time. But you have to look ahead. I mean you have to keep hoping you're going to find a way out.

"You just can't lie here and condemn yourself to a life behind bars, even if others have condemned you to that.

"I read everything I can get my hands on. Some time ago I got involved in a mail course in IBM computer programming. I'm even doing some weight-lifting and exercise. Mastrian is trying to get me to jog. I'll take the weights. I couldn't get halfway up to the bar on my first tries at pull-ups last year. I go up and down like a Yo-yo now."

The reference was to Norman Mastrian, also serving a life term in the Thompson case as the middleman in the killing. Mastrian dwells on the main floor of the prison's honor D block, reserved for prisoners who stay out of institutional trouble. Thompson is celled in one of the upper galleries of the same block.

In the prison community, Thompson stays relatively detached, although he is not anti-social. Mastrian is the happiness boy of the institution, a Kiwanian type among killers, arsonists, thieves and sodomists. He is talkative and plausible, an operator. Guards like him and so do most of the inmates.

A few hours earlier I had run ten laps around the inner prison compound, or "yard," with him, awash in sweat from 90-degree heat. Mastrian is convinced he is going to get a new trial, that the whole case against him will be exposed some day as a political and legal conspiracy.

"In the meantime," he says, "I make do around here. I stay in shape—run, lift weights, play basketball. I'm forty-five. I feel great. Why do I want to be hang-dog? I kill the time by exercising myself into exhaustion. Do I like it here? Hell no. But I'm not going to accept being buried forever."

Mastrian is a muscle beacher among the cons, very much proud of his chest expansion, biceps and stamina. He could make it on a television exercise show today as the successor to Jack LaLanne. He is also an expert on diet, and lectures the flabby-gut starch victims around him on the wisdom of protein eating.

Thompson is no such evangelist.

"I suppose they come to me every day for some advice on how to handle their legal trouble," he says. "I have a rule on that. I listen if they don't have an attorney. If they have something to work on, I'll tell them, maybe suggest how they should seek legal help outside. Once in a rare while I'll work with them if there is a case where their conviction obviously can be set aside. But there are rules in here about those things, and you have to live with the institution."

He wanted to talk about the law. But his caution hung up a flag here. He was a lawyer before his conviction, and he must have viewed the law then from the stance of a successful professional who was confident in it and not necessarily overburdened by the inequities with which it may actually be practiced.

He now is serving a life term for murder, and the law is the only thing that can ever get him off. It takes no overpowering insight to recognize that he is impatient and galled now by legal delays and bush-beating which, as a practicing lawyer, he might have considered normal and unavoidable.

He does not say all of these things, but it is clear that he feels them. It is one thing for an attorney to practice law, party with the other boys and judges, and to take one case at a time in a good and established tempo.

It is another thing altogether to be an ex-attorney facing an eternity behind bars, aware about time-stretching due process and paper bureaucracy.

On the street, it might be something the attorney shrugs about at 5:30 on his way home from work.

But in prison it is something he must rage about inwardly—if he has any remaining hook on which to hang his case—because there is no going home at 5:30 p.m.

"I can't deny I look at the law from a different viewpoint now," he says. "Does it really protect? Is it the impersonal thing, free of politics and emotion, that a lot of Americans were taught to believe, or is this a myth?"

He is solemn and quietly passionate when he talks about this. But you remind yourself about the jury system, and verdicts, and that he stands convicted of a ghastly crime, and what right does he have to question the process by which he flourished and which then exiled him.

But he does have the right, of course, on technical grounds if nothing else. And, the judgment already having been made, there is no need for his visitor to make it all over.

"On the record," I say, "it is hard for a man to sympathize with you. There are other things for which he should reserve his sympathy."

"What," he says, "if justice was not done?"

We leave it there. We are not re-trying the case.

"I spoke about holding onto your personality," he says. "This is an unnatural environment but you don't want to surrender your curiosity.

"Otherwise you're going to become part of the walls, corridors, language, the routine. When I first got here I didn't use the language the others use. I know they figured me as an oddball. Gradually you have to use some of it, the slang, the rough stuff, because this is how you have to communicate here. I'm not trying to hold myself completely apart. But you have to try to keep a grip on some of the things you associate with normal society."

He has been visited by his son, a college student. The prison having installed a new, comfortable reception room he hopes now to have visits from his three daughters.

Some of the convicts in the society around him view him with disapproval, or envy, but to the majority he appears to be "okay, he don't bother you none."

His relationships with prison authority are uneventful. Aside from the few institutional luxuries his money has given him, he enjoys no particular status in this polarized world, where a man's worth is not measured by his background or the kind of time he is doing, but by his reliability and apparent character.

And yet the watchword here is "trust nobody with the big things, the things about yourself that mean a damn."

This is a maximum security prison. To hear the prison spokesman tell it, it is viewed favorably by national penal experts. To hear the cell block sociologists inside tell it, it is still ten years behind the times in creature comforts, vocational training, medical care.

Almost everybody behind bars here belongs here. Some

have been maltreated by erratic law and sloppy legal administration in the courts. Twenty years ago prisoners were beaten routinely, gassed, left to rot. Today there is little, if any, brutality. The relationship between con and guard is chummy at times, and as long as you do not throw it in the sergeant's face you can gamble whenever you want. If you're really lucky you might get some booze.

And once in a great while, if you're in the farm colony and the stars are with you, you might dally with a woman.

The average American's view of penitentiary life springs not from parole board transcripts but from the studios of Metro-Goldwyn-Mayer.

The convict is Burt Lancester wearing gray prison woolens, billed cap and flaring nostrils; his antagonist the sadistic and politically fearful warden. There are bullying guards, slop for food and escape conspiracies culminating when Lancaster runs a truck through the prison gates, leaves four dead convicts behind and dies in the arms of the warden's daughter, who used to smuggle hot biscuits into solitary.

The role does not bear much resemblance to Minnesota's Stillwater Prison of today.

Twenty years ago, it may not have been so far-fetched, with the exception that there has never been a succssful escape from within the walls of the maximum security penitentiary.

One resourceful convict scored a near miss a few years ago, when, on a densely overcast day, he knotted three or four strands of rope from the twine shop and attached a baling hook to the end.

As the fog descended to ground level, he walked into

the prison compound within fifty feet of a gun tower, flung the hook to the top of the 28-foot wall and, with a Cornell Wilde vault to Valhalla, scaled the wall as the sentries sat around, oblivious.

At this point he was overcome by caution and spent the next couple of hours hiding out in the bushes, from which he was plucked by the guards and returned to quarters.

Life in the Minnesota state prison today, however, is not so uncivilized as to spawn escape plots wholesale or stir do-or-die showdowns between desperate convicts and black-guard screws. There aren't many of either description left.

"If you gotta have the truth," said a laryngitic old lifer, "it ain't a helluva lot different than a playpen compared with the dungeon it used to be."

The lifer has made his peace with the prison. He is content now, or as content as it is possible to be within the society of walls and bars and cellblock gates. There are younger men here who rail at the remnants of the old system when a con was an animal without rights or much hope.

This is a man we can call Jonesy, who lives on the prison's farm colony and who will soon be paroled to a good job. He is tanned, lean, intelligent, profane. He has spent two decades of his forty-four years behind bars, most of them in Stillwater prison.

"Since 1940," he says, "close to thirty years, I guess I never earned more than $11,000 when it was all figured up, and I may be cheating about that. I never had a Social Security card. The reason was that all my life I'd rather steal the stuff than work for it, and if I didn't have a good job offer from a friend I suppose I'd steal again.

"One of the reasons is that when you get out, unless you're really lucky or know somebody, you just ain't got enough money and can't get a decent job, so you go back to doing what you used to do. I was paroled a couple of years ago. I tried like hell, but the best I could do was $63 a week. How are you going to make it on that?

"But I'll tell you what this place has done to me, it used to be horrible, a hell pit. They used to hit you with a cane, and never let you talk, and if you did something wrong they threw you in the hole and hung you up on the doors with chains and just beat the hell out of you if you tried to be a man and tell them what they were.

"I tried to kill myself once, with a razor."

He rolled up his khaki shirt sleeve to disclose stitch-work the width of his wrist.

"I didn't die, but at least it was a change.

"Nobody around here used to believe you could be human to a con without sacrificing your manhood or whatever the guards were afraid to sacrifice. Then they actually started thinking about the con as though he was a man. Now you people use fancy language like penal reform and therapy and justice and humanity, but that's how it all comes out to a con.

"After years in this rat hole, I was a man again.

"I believed them. Even the warden's assistant I used to hate and thought was a lying bastard. He started treating me like a man. So I got no more troubles here, and I'm getting out and I'm getting a good job because I'm lucky and maybe I got just one break coming.

"Will I stay out of trouble you ask? I think so. But I been in this place too long and seen too many come back to make a helluva big bet on it."

There is always a hazard in classifying living conditions in an institution like Stillwater, whose population is a horizontal slice of society's rebels, misfits and unfortunates. An outsider viewing it for four days can hardly arrive at valid conclusions or even tentative ones on most of the sides to prison life. He may talk to the ax-grinders, from the cop to the staff lieutenant, and walk away feeling like a sponge.

On the other hand, one does not have to watch a fire for five years to realize it is burning.

The prison takes care of the physical needs of its inmates, beyond much dispute. It feeds, clothes and exercises its people well. It allows them to move around in the yard and cellblocks with reasonable dignity and it condones petty gambling on a rather elaborate scale.

It also winks at some of the minor league dodges—such as thievery from the kitchen or the dining room—in the interest of amiable relations between the con and the watchdog. It does this in the hard-headed realization that there is some larceny and gaming spirit in the heart of almost everybody.

"The prison regulations say the convicts can't gamble," one of the old-line officers said. "But you got to take a pretty broad view of human nature. You put three ministers and a priest on an island and in a couple of days, after everybody's soul has been saved, they'll probably break out a deck of cards.

"Yeah, yeah, we know how they do all the gambling on baseball and football pools and using cribbage boards to count the bets in card games that aren't supposed to be low-ball poker but are. And they gamble with cigarettes, and the legal limit on cartons in one cell is five, but the winners spread them around so that the non-smokers keep them for them.

"And there is some illegal cash money in here; they call it green, and a con's wife may slip it into his mouth pretending they are kissing goodbye passionately in the visiting room. But it's rough on them if they're caught with money or booze, which also gets in here sometime."

The conduits in this high-wall form of bootlegging are referred to as "horses," prison employes or guards who are paid to bring in the contraband. The evidence indicates that traffic in liquor at the prison is minimal and not serious. Now and then some overnight hootch may be concocted in the kitchen or in one of the industrial plants where there is some basic equipment for fermentation.

"Most of the stuff that gets in here," the officer said, "comes in around Christmas. Anybody get caught, he goes into the tank. But we don't consider it a serious problem. The gambling, on the other hand, is pretty widespread. As long as we don't see any open evidence of it—I mean the collecting of cigarette cartons or passing of money— we don't do too much snooping. If it gets flagrant, we crack down."

On a midweek day during which I strolled around the prison's honor block, which houses four or five score of its model prisoners, there were at least three baseball pools in active and technically illegal operation.

I scanned one handed me by a genial long-termer. It was tidily typed, listing the day's major league opponents and the odds. If you picked four of four winners out of the nine possibilities that day, you won eight packages of cigarettes for each one you wagered. If you picked five out of five, you won twelve for one.

"All the games," the bookie said, "are even today except I'm handicapping Cleveland one run—they've pitching Tiant today—and St. Louis one run."

Our trails crossed the following morning. "How'd you do yesterday," I asked. "I won thirty-three packs," he said. "I was right on the nose on St. Louis and Cleveland. Both of them won by a run, which means it's a tie and kills the bettor."

"Congratulations," I said.

"Save it," he replied. "I'm about to lose all my winnings playing poker."

Little of this seems to damage the edge of prison discipline. The cons understand the psychology all right, that the prison administration sees the wisdom of letting them have the carrot stick as a pacifier.

The obvious violators wind up in a disciplinary session termed "court" wherein prison officials try and judge alleged offenses against the prison code.

One is in progress today, beginning shortly after noon. We are visitors here, so there is no point in pretending the proceedings and language are typical, but they are close enough.

There are only two cases, both petty. One of the inmates is charged with refusing to pour coffee in the dining room, pleading that he has a medical certificate placing him on light duty. He has a reputation for being a crybaby and shirker. The presiding judge is Capt. Mike Eckerstrom, a hard-talking, unsmiling black-haired Navy combat veteran. He has the respect of the inmates as a tough but fair and totally realistic prison officer.

Eckerstrom gets this inmate transferred to another job, rather disdainfully.

Another young convict, stocky and reticent, enters the office, charged with eating in the shortline reserved for special work details at 10:30 a.m. and another full meal at twelve noon. "Is that correct?" the captain asks.

"Yes."

"Why."

"I was hungry," the inmate replies with unflankable logic.

They let him off with a warning and the inmate vows it won't happen again, and Eckerstrom releases him to his cell block with the rather intimate epilogue: "Okay, Freddie, now please don't forget what you are saying because if you do it's your ass."

Freddie's home is one of the standard maximum security

cells in Cell Block B. He lives by himself there when he and three hundred fity or so industrial laborers (twine, farm machinery, foundry) aren't working their daily shifts for an average of sevently cents a day, or taking recreation out in the compound in the evening, or watching television in the corridor.

His cell is on the lower level of four galleries, equipped with a cot, sink, toilet bowl, a utility cabinet on the wall in which he has some sweets bought from the canteen, and a plug-in radio from which he can listen by earphones to his choice of four stations—WCCO, KTCI, KSTP and WJSW Stillwater.

I check in for the night with my basket of prison clothes and shaving kit. "I see," my neighbor says, "they issued you your depravity kit." I nod. "What happened to you," I ask.

The convicts don't object sharing their troubles. "I'm one of the guys who wanted things faster than he could afford," the man said. "I started out easy with a couple of small banks. The last one was a big supermarket with a warning system.

"I should have stuck to banks."

Horror at Haiti

One of the small but melancholy sagas of our generation — an all-male gambling junket to Haiti that began in Minneapolis and ended in calamity — has just come to light today and deserves your undivided condolences.

It was related to me by one of the victims, a young Minneapolis lawyer named John Bix, who cannot decide whether to blame the influence of Haitian voodoo or shaved dice.

As a student of life's little convulsions, I listened to his sad narrative with growing wonderment. At length I concluded that here was the culminating agony in the long, soap-opera history of the vacation-gone-wrong. In honor of the narrator, we will call it John's Other Strife.

"Gulled by the honied phrases of a Caribbean brochure," Bix began, "about 125 Twin Cities business types signed on. The deal was that for $550 we got everything for five days — the jet plane transportation, deluxe rooms, food and $500 worth of gambling chips. Which meant that we were supposedly getting the whole thing for $50, depending on what happened at the casino.

"Well, there were people like Ted Vickerman, Ken Fischman, Gunnar Rovick, Ray Duffy, Ted Vusich, Jerry Mayeron — all clean-cut, fun-seeking Twin Citians, the flower of the community. We were to fly to Miami and then to Haiti en masse.

"Saturday night, February 17, half of us got calls from the local promoter telling us there wasn't room for every-

body on the charter, and some would have to go commercial.

"I was on the commercial, which got to Miami in
midmorning. About eleven o'clock a scruffy, unshaved
character showed up and said he was representing our
hosts in Haiti and would arrange planes to Haiti, six
hundred miles away.

"He said he would get two DC-3's, the two-engine
planes that were built before the American Revolution,
from Lauderdale. It got to be two o'clock, four o'clock,
seven o'clock. He says now that he can't get the planes
tonight, and we will have to stay over.

"But there aren't any hotel rooms, he says.

"We find a place, the 75 of us, called the Biscayne. The
only place for us is the hotel ballroom. They wheel in cots.
We haul our luggage and golf bags and booze in. There's
only one bathroom and no shower, and the bathroom is
seven floors down. There's no elevator. I mean, friend,
some of these guys in this group are the big-rollers, $75,000
a year, and it's a helluva comedown to spend your first
night of a luxury vacation in a flophouse.

"We are back at the terminal at 9:00 a.m., now twenty-
four hours late on our idyl in the Caribbean, grimy, unshaved and hung over. The guy says he still has no planes.
We find out his office is his beat-up old Chevy and his
operations headquarters is the telephone booth.

"The DC-3's arrive at 3:00 p.m. One of the pilots is
drinking from a Coke bottle with booze in it, and I hear
him say, 'How do you get this old goose off the ground?'

"But somehow he does. The plane has got no food, no
ventillation, no stewardesses. They guy next to me tried
to strap in, and the strap came out in his hand. He settled
back, and the seat toppled over.

"We get to Haiti, and the hotel where they tried to put

up the first contingent from the other Minneapolis plane is not the Castle Haiti Hotel in Port-au-Prince as advertised, but a dive so bad our people refused to walk in the door. Later we got relocated near a place where they raise roosters for cock-fighting. The noise of the crowing cocks is deafening, drowning out the surf, which you can't see anyhow because of the swamp where there was supposed to be a beach.

"That night at the gambling table we find out they are not going to cash our chips for money, if we want it that way, but let us go the whole four days taking any winnings in chips and nothing else. For four days they don't change the black jack deck.

"Vickerman, who won the Minnesota amateur a few years ago, wants to play golf, but there's no course. The only one is forty miles away at the American embassy. He rides over rocky mountain roads to get there, but then can't play because the ride has twisted his back out of shape, and he spends the next three days in his hotel room.

"You remember my telling you the whole package cost $550, of which $500 was given back to us in Haiti in the form of gambling chips.

"There were a few sharpies who figured they would cash the chips immediately and come out miles ahead. No dice, friend, not even crooked dice. It got so that the chips were next to worthless. I was selling mine at a few cents on the dollar.

"Finally on the last day they let us trade them in on the checks deposited with the gamblers by the really big losers in our group. By this time I'm out of it, having thrown most of my chips into the ocean.

"I asked one guy what was the name of the little Port-au-Prince suburb where we were gambling and it has a romantic ring in Spanish but in English it is translated

Pigeonville. I swear to heaven that's the name.

"It gets to be Thursday, the day we have to leave, and nobody is walking around with the bronze, he-man Caribbean tan we were looking for. We figured we would come back with character in our faces, but all we got is bloodshot eyes and beige complexions from getting stuck in too many elevators that didn't work and too many bars that did.

"The creole food was nourishing but extremely flammable, so that half of us have got dysentery and the other half are constipated.

"They tell us we are going to depart Thursday afternoon, some of us on the two DC-3's to Florida and the others on a jet charter coming from Seattle.

"The first guy the DC-3 passengers see at the terminal is the thirsty pilot about whom I told you. He is big-shouldered, handsome, swashbuckling type who looks like Victor Mature but drinks like Phil Harris. He has a bottle of eight-year-old Grant's Scotch in his hand, and he says he doesn't see how the plane is supposed to take off today. Each time we see him take a pull from the Grant's he looks like a better prophet.

"The reason he is dubious is that the pilots haven't been paid; the hotel hasn't been paid, and the ground crews haven't been paid. Plus, nobody has paid for the airplane fuel. The promoter who arranged the tour from Minneapolis is near tears and he takes it on the lam to New York. We are in danger of being marrooned in Haiti, so there is nothing else to do but take up a collection among the passengers. We pass the hat and raise $700 for fuel, the pilots and the crews.

"The Victor Mature-type gets his plane off the ground, but bounces back down and then in one graceful leap he vaults the mountains before evidently passing out and relinquishing the controls to the co-pilot.

"I'm on the other DC-3, which is airborne just a couple of minutes when Ken Fischman leans over to me and says, 'I don't know about you, but I swear the left propeller isn't turning.' What it is, we have blown a rod and have to land. The other DC-3 gets to Florida.

"We wait for the charter jet, which we hear is not going to be able to land at night in Haiti because Papa Doc Duvalier, the dictator, is afraid of revolutionary activity and doesn't want to turn on the airport landing lights.

"Guys are now trying to get out of Haiti commercially. I know people who had to get back to Minneapolis by way of London. One guy calls his wife and says something, in his half-shot condition, about not being able to talk, that he will contact her later, if he can get out.

"She concludes we are under some kind of siege in Haiti, gets in touch with Senator Mondale's office, and says something about a firing squad. Well, the jet finally gets clearance to land in the early morning. We charge out to the plane deliriously, like children let in free at the circus. And we are home. Home, friend, home!"

Vacantly, Bix fingered a jagged wood-carving. "It cost $25 in a Haitian souvenir shop," he said. "I bought it as mahogany. It cracked when I stepped off the ramp at Wold."

And Now the Reverend Rests

W hen a good man dies, it is the human and traditional thing for his friends, admirers and colleagues to lay upon his memory a language of reverence meant to honor him and to acknowledge our debt to his works.

It is then when we realize, however, in the death of a man so remarkable and towering as the Reverend Dr. Reuben Youngdahl, how arid and faceless the language of the eulogy can be, because there is no way for it to translate the vitality, the light earthiness and the hand-to-hand friendship by which thousands in his congregation and other thousands outside of it knew him.

The reverend was a man apart, the athlete-pastor, the philosopher-pastor, the politician-pastor, the capitalist-pastor, the visionary-pastor. He built a vast congregation of ten thousand at Mount Olivet Lutheran Church and was a confidante of some of the decision-makers of the world, but many of his followers remember him best and most affectionately going from door to door in a windbreaker, hustling memberships in his church.

He had a genius for communication, not necessarily as a sermonizer or writer but in the face-to-face dialogue of the church lawn and coffee party. Without their realizing it, perhaps, for thousands in his church he removed the gray beard from God and replaced this image with a picture of a buoyant and companionable God, as intimate at a picnic or in the board room as in church.

As much as it was practical or possible, he lived by his creed — that the individual should pack his life to the fullest with meaningful action and thought; that while you might get to heaven by being purely reverential, this did not necessarily help the crippled kids in town or the impoverished widows.

And so he built camps and hospitals and clinics and funds. As a mover, a manager, he was relentless. "The guy," a church worker said yesterday, "conned me out of hundreds of hours of my time, which, of course, also meant a lot of money. It wasn't that I objected to the extra church work, but I'm like most people who usually have something better to do with their time. Without offending, he made you think about what you were really saying when you tried to beg off, and you always wound up giving him your time. And it wasn't Reuben Youngdahl you were giving the time to at all, of course, but sometimes it was best for him to make it seem that way."

In many ways he was the essence of the Lutheran ethic, seasoning his faith with a large measure of practical good works which, in the aftermath of Reuben Youngdahl's life, will be enduring in this community. He could move his congregation on Sunday mornings but his was perhaps not the classic pulpitry of precise and carefully reasoned theology. The reverend dealt with people. To many of them he was less a witness than a friend.

There are hospital aides in town who knew that the best kind of therapy for some of their patients was nothing the doctor could give them, but rather a two-minute visit with Reuben Youngdahl — especially the patients who were going to die soon and must have known it.

"He had a way," a woman with terminal cancer told a visitor, "of making you want to live again. He was so full of life, and he didn't have to say inspirational things to get you out of your depression. He just kidded you out of feeling sorry for yourself. And he always had a strong grip for your wrist."

It was as appropriate to see Reuben Youngdahl in a football stadium or a board meeting as it was in the church or clinic. He knew the language of the clubhouse, and he did not blush when the athletic society around him got a little roistering. There were big name athletes and figures who came annually to his Sportsman's Dinner, but there was rarely much doubt who was the man among men in the crowd.

"Death," he said in his last book, "is not easy. It is so unwelcome to many that they prefer to ignore it. They dismiss the possibility with an attitude of 'it can't happen to me.' But someday when it strikes close we are jolted into the realities of how uncertain is our time in this life."

No man could have done more with the time in his life. The hundreds who knew him from the sportsman's table will join his congregation in remembering: "There went a man."

Society's Safety Valve

It is now abundantly clear that if Joe Kapp did not exist he would have to be invented, society's buffer against some of the great psychotic dilemmas of our time.

The situation was explained to me at Metropolitan Stadium Sunday by a prosperous psychiatrist from Bloomington, who spends six days a week disarranging the love lives of suburban housewives and who soothes his own jangled nerves viewing Kapp and the Vikings on Sundays.

"Each society, in its own time and its own crises, walks a thin line between stability and hysteria," he said. "The Twin Cities, as a matter of fact these 47,000 people here today, are society in miniature. They are beset by problems crowding in on them, harassed by bill collectors, confused by clothes designers who want them to change their sex, offended by experts who tell them how they are going to vote and chagrined because nobody wants to listen to them on how to end Vietnam. They not only need but absolutely demand a Joe Kapp to prevent them from going over the wall."

"I'm glad Joe is so therapeutic for you and the others," I intervened, "because he's already got me halfway over the side and the Vikings don't even have the ball."

"Exactly. Your problems are more imagined than real. As the team is presently constituted, you don't really have to worry about Dallas scoring until the Vikings go on offense.

"It must be obvious to you that Kapp is playing well and bravely, but unfortunately on the three or four plays when he goes bad he is breath-takingly bad. And that on these occasions when he fouls up the play he does it with such originality and so publicly he achieves that rare psychological slam—both provoking the audience and confusing the Cowboys. Accordingly, Dallas' first impulse is not to pass to the world's fastest human but to surrender the ball on the spot and let fate and Joe take over."

"No one man," I said, out of the depths of loyalty for Kapp, "has the kind of metaphysical power to unhinge everybody in the stadium at once, in so many directions. Only the public address announcer at the University of Minnesota games has that kind of versatility."

By common consent we fell silent to view Joe's latest agonies on the field, and to monitor some of the reaction of his mortified public in the stands.

"All you need Joe," a man behind us screamed, "is one more training camp to learn the Viking offense. When that happens, we're all sunk. That's right, Joe, two touchdowns behind and you call a handoff. Way to run out the clock, Joe baby.

"Keep your mouth shut, Mac," a voice rasped nearby, "you want Joe to call a pass?"

The psychiatrist nudged me, as though to confirm his diagnosis. "All of us need some symbolic object against whom we may vent our antagonisms, our sense of superiority, our feeling of lofty contempt. Watching Joe throw a pass up there in the troposphere when he is rushed, we develop a common bond of vague, if affectionate, mass disdain. In this respect, Joe Kapp is the Spam of the 1960s."

"Doc," I said, "all we want to do is put Joe in the end zone, not in a tin can."

"Nevertheless, he serves the same psychological purpose for us. Now you and I know the Vikings probably were not ready to handle as much blitzing as Dallas is doing, and the offensive line has had better games, and so has the backfield, but now there is Joe catapulting the football way up in the air, and if that ball comes down, brother, we have got troubles."

We follow the erratic flight of the ball in quiet horror, and then observe the unusual action of two Dallas defensive backs. They are flipping coins to see which of the two will intercept. This is not entirely unprecedented. But I mean TWO OUT OF THREE?

And yet somebody with the soul of Solomon arranges for the interceptor to fumble the ball to our men, and it is one of the Vikings' more successful maneuvers of the day. Kapp now runs. He seems always to be one step ahead of the linebacker and a half step ahead of collapse, but he always gains, and fortunately, the linebacker always gets him first. He now keeps the drive going by shot-putting a pass, off balance and moving in the wrong direction. To thousands among us he looks like a left-handed butcher cutting a rump roast with his arm in a sling.

But they score. The fellow has nerve, but he does not have much support today and gives us the distinct impression that he is playing the game under reprieve.

"The fans," I told the psychiatrist, "are booing Joe. How do you think it would have gone with him if he were in with the Christians and lions 2,000 years ago?"

"The way Joe is going," he said, "he could spear all the lions and still lose the broad, who is no doubt back at the spa recuperating from the gout."

Marriage on a Credit Card

News last week that the once-sedate Dayton's department store is going to start selling booze with its buffets left the market world aflutter and a few of the little old lady shoppers appalled.

Today, however, with the discovery that Dayton's has now gone into the electronic dating business, we have evidence that this truly astounding institution has finally broken through all cosmic barriers. As an influence on our lives and fortunes, it has now passed the Internal Revenue Service and the auto body shops, and drawn even with Cal Griffith.

For $6 — discounted, of course, from the regular price — Dayton's guarantees it will provide you with the names and telephone numbers of at least two and possibly ten or twenty people who are potential lovemates. These, presumably, can either fulfill your destiny or put you in court, depending on how well the computer's cog wheels are oiled.

What this means as a practical matter is that only the S-A service stations can now match Dayton's in the diversity of its merchandise. Dayton's began by selling shoes, shirts and piety. Gradually it expanded to fur coats and cars. It now offers the ultimate in full service such as seminars on dieting, how to mix drinks and this month a mechanized system of finding a mate.

In other words, Dayton's can get you juiced, reduced and seduced on the same credit card.

You are aware how the computer works. You fill out

a profile card which bares your most intimate secrets to the machine's condensors. Omnisciently, the machine knows you are lying when you describe your looks as above average, because there are questions later on that betray your deceit, such as, "Are you cool or involved," and "Are you a rabbit or a turtle?"

"What happens," I asked one of Dayton's public relations people, "if you are a speckled grouse?"

"Dayton's," she said, "is simply staying in tune with the times. This is February, love month. Lovers, as people, are fascinated by machines. The computer will take their profile card and match it with a person of the opposite sex who may be compatible. Dayton's obviously does not guarantee a marriage but it does guarantee some possibilities.

"By this I mean telephonic, or through the mail. What develops after this does interest us, of course, because married people tend to shop and I can't think of a better place to shop than Dayton's.

"This computer dating system is not intended for the noodniks of romance, the chronic losers, as some people suggest. What it tries to do is to give the unmarried person, young or old, some power of selection, to avoid accidentally getting tied up with a henpecking mate."

What is does then, is produce a choice, not a heckle?

"Well, yes. Actually, it's the One Plus One company that handles the operation. We're merchandising it here this month on our second floor. The company's regular rates are $7.50 for three months. For this you get at least two names every two weeks, with an option to renew the service at $5 for the next three months. Considering the potential of the merchandise, our reduced rate of $6 is not a bad over-the-counter value."

In the spirit of the times, the machine's psychiatrists

give you maximum range to classify yourself at the outset, listing under identification by sex these options: "(1) Male (2) Female (3) Other."

Off the record, the computer's analysts will confirm what men have suspected through the ages, that there is more vanity among women. One question, for example, asks the respondent to evaluate his lovemaking prowess — "(1) Fine, indeed (2) Adequate (3) Slightly Cold."

"While a slight majority of men described themselves as fine," one of the informants noted, "fully eighty per cent of the women gave themselves the highest grade in this significant category. It is difficult to explain."

"The explanation," a woman shopper volunteered, "is that the ratings are undoubtedly correct."

At the moment the company has about two thousand names on its active file. The most active is a 72-year-old widower who already has gone through thirty names and may soon be taken off the board. "We have had only one request for a service call," the analyst said mysteriously, "from a woman in Rochester."

Unquestionably, the Dayton's corporation will stand behind all of the liaisons it is going to create and I'm sure will allow full credit for alimony payments when the machine goes on the fritz.

I think the system has considerable merit, but my best advice to the uncommitted bachelor at this point is to take his chances at Murray's piano bar.

Riddle of the Portable Mattress

We have before us today one of the provocative riddles of the week's Minneapolis police blotter: The case of the unidentified woman last seen in the entrance of the Radisson Hotel carrying a mattress.

There are elements of mystery and suspense in this that make it a worthy subject for speculation, a time for us to ponder the great, unexplained forces that would impel a woman into this baffling act.

"Would you say," my informant at the Radisson observed, "that she was being a little too obvious if she were really a prostitute?"

"That is correct," I agreed. "Streetwalkers nowadays in Minneapolis have attained a detached, businesslike attitude toward their work and as a rule do not take the cares and the trappings of the office home with them.

"Further, there simply is not much precedent for that kind of commerce among Minneapolis streetwalkers, who would generally regard the carrying of a mattress as a form of unethical advertising.

"In addition, there is nothing on the record in the files of the Minneapolis morals squad or the municipal courts to indicate this might be a new modus operandi for the girls. A week ago, you will recall, Judge Wolner pointed out we have records showing cases of dalliance in boatels, automobiles, motels, self-paddling kayaks and semi-trailers, but there is not a single substantiated case of any swell being tempted locally by an open-air Sealy."

And so I was disappointed to learn of the Victorian

prudery and jitteriness with which the responsible people handled this case.

The facts are brief and quickly recited. The police radio at 5:55 a.m. Wednesday reported a sighting from downtown Minneapolis, a woman in the doorway of the Radisson, carrying a fully-lined, apparently all-springed, name-brand mattress.

"What," I asked one of the night men at the Radisson, "was so unusual about that?"

"The mattress," he explained, "tended to get wedged in the doorway and was distracting some of our early-morning arrivals, plus it was making the woman top-heavy and in danger of capsizing."

Witnesses reported the woman was of an age that might range from thirty to forty or so.

"Did she look as though she needed assistance, or money, or warm beer?" I asked.

"She looked," he said, "as though she needed some sleep."

And now, of course, we are getting to the marrow of it: "What is so bizarre about a woman at a hotel needing sleep at 5:55 in the morning with a mattress so nearby?"

"Because," he replied, "it was impossible to know whether she wanted to register, solicit, homestead, sweep out or ask for an oil job for her springs. Accordingly, the incident was reported to the police routinely."

I persisted, maintaining we had a classic case of impending police brutality here, an impingement on the American woman's long-standing and bitterly-won right to stand in a hotel doorway with a mattress at 5:55 in the morning.

"What was she going to be charged with?" I demanded. He hesitated.

"There is no documented instance," I reminded him,

"of a woman being convicted of exposing a posture-pedic. I doubt there is such a charge. I know for an absolute certainty you are never going to get a jury to accept it."

Officers Wilbur Eck and R. D. Gardner were summoned, however, and discovered with some relief that the woman was gone. She had disappeared into the darkness to the east in the direction of the Nicollet Mall, where she will achieve a merciful obscurity on that whirling ferris wheel of commerce and indomitable kooks.

But what of her background, the human drama, perhaps the small, casual tragedy in her life that put her in the airflow of the Radisson doorway with an all-spring mattress? We may conjecture, but nothing more.

Maybe all it was, her husband snores.

Toonerville Airport in the Pines

Once or twice annually I fly to my home town of Ely on the Iron Range to give my father an accounting of my stewardship in the vast metropolis here. I do this to congratulate myself on my progress since I left the fresh air, the uncongested roads and the unpolluted lakes and streams.

I suppose it should be explained that putting an airplane down on the airport at Ely is not so much a landing as an act of faith. The field is bound tightly by a highway on the west, a pine grove on the south, a high tension line on the east and a cemetery on the north.

"We have the only airport on the Range," the field's manager tells me, "where when the navigator uses the term 'dead reckoning,' he means it literally."

The field is situated on a shifting muskeg swamp and is therefore a favorite of Navy fliers, who are accustomed to landing on moving runways and who fondly refer to the Ely field as the country's most inland aircraft carrier.

To the small plane pilot, the runways present the double delight of being not only soggy but short. Three times a year in Ely they conduct gala, bring-your-own-refreshments dredging parties where they scoop for unreported Cessnas in the bogs at the end of runways.

"The last time we dug," a dredger advised me, "we went so far one of the legislators got all excited and proposed a bill establishing a special tax exemption for propeller exploration. He contended the territory has vast, unplumbed reserves of magnetoes and gyro compasses in the rich virgin swamps adjacent to the airport.

"I expect the legislature to buy it, just like they bought the weepy stories about the taconite amendment and the even weepier ones from the guys who said they were going to mine nickel here but never did. So I think you can expect Mr. Rosenmeier and his friends to put through the propeller amendment next year, not necessarily to help the propellers but just to re-confirm the lawmakers' profound interest in things that go around in circles."

I quickly squelched the political talk, however: "Tell me about landing on this little airport from the northeast," I said.

"Well, this is one of the last great refuges of the bush pilot, but as you can see you have problems there from Cemetery Hill, which is about 500 feet higher than the runway—503 or 504 if you allow for some of the bigger headstones. This can be overcome.

"Do not get complacent, however, because right in the middle of the final approach there you will see that ski scaffold. We have the only airfield in the state where the pilot has to be an experienced slalom rider in order to escape disaster."

"Are there any other geographic notes to relieve the boredom of landing here," I asked.

"Well, yes. From the southeast approach there. You will notice the power lines practically on the edge of the runway. Because of their location the people around here say the pilot usually has his option, I mean he can either go over the lines or under them."

"IS THERE ANY CHANCE," I asked hopefully, of going BETWEEN the wires?"

"Only," he said, "if the wind is favorable and you have retractable landing gear."

To shortening the account, I should tell you I had no

trouble landing but needed to call the American Hoist and Derrick people to assist with my take-off.

From a sociological standpoint, I suppose, I should relate the gist of my conversation with my father, who has spent his lifetime on the Range in the woodland, the mines and the fishing streams.

"Tell me, father," I said, "What is new in the wilderness?"

"It used to be that you could tell the tourist by the orange life preserver he wore in the taverns and the metropolitan way that he swatted the mosquitoes," he said. "Now they all walk around with 14-foot aluminum canoes on their heads and call themselves voyageurs. But they are good people and no doubt the salvation of the north. How is the wilderness coming in the Twin Cities?"

"Very suspenseful, the life," I said eagerly, "although a little different from the Ely wilderness. In the Twin Cities when you go swimming you are either going to be purged or poisoned. As for the traffic problems, resourceful drivers reduce the chance of being gassed by periodically ignoring all of the arrows and driving down into the street excavations, where the air is dustier but has a lower monoxide content."

"You sure you don't want to stay here a little longer?" he asked.

"No," I said gravely, "the place just doesn't have enough, well, style."

The Stubborn Prophet of Medicine Lake

With you, I was startled and dismayed to discover in The Minneapolis Star's latest Metro-Poll the low estate into which bartenders have fallen in the advice-giving dodge.

Periodically, The Star puts a stethoscope on the public to find what — besides sex — motivates people, angers them, bankrupts them and titillates them. We do this in order better to serve our audience in Starland and to pinpoint for the more controversial authors the likely sites of land mine emplacements and bear traps laid by wrathful readers.

In this newest survey, readers were asked to rate professional and service people who frequently come into contact with the small, daily agonies of their customers. The idea was for the pollees to indicate which they trusted most, which they trusted least and which simply bore watching.

Digested, the results tell us 94 per cent of the people think they get good advice from parents, 73 per cent think we get good advice from doctors, 70 per cent from dentists, 67 per cent from clergymen, 52 per cent from bankers, 51 per cent from lawyers, 24 per cent from barbers or beauticians, and only 11 per cent from cab drivers and 10 per cent from bartenders.

Jarred by this, I hastened to one of my favorite all-around, if unregistered authorities, Bob Winters, proprietor of the Apple Blossom Inn on Medicine Lake. Winters originated in the Klondike and has the gnarled, skeptical and historically battered facial features of a man who not only took part in the Gold Rush but got run over by it.

Winters is the kind of prophet to whom you must go whenever a thought strikes you with such absolute, glass-like clarity that it simply needs a little confusion to make it respectable. This Winters normally provides. Today, however, he appeared saddened by results of the poll, listing bartenders as the least reliable of the occupational geniuses.

"The trouble with the world," he said at length, "is that there's just too damn much advice in it. We are advised how to have sex and how not to have it, what to eat and what not to eat. We are told how to drive in the winter, and then told to stay the hell off the streets.

"Now, I used to have my own ratings on where the best advice came from, and the clergymen were always right up there, usually going for No. 1 or at least a tie. But now we get ministers who tell us God is dead and we get priests who get married, so it's tough to tell who is going to have a rougher time getting into heaven, the congregations or the clergymen."

Winters peered at me thoughtfully, and it was clear that what he would say next would attempt to be helpful without really being slanderous. "The newspapers and radio stations give you advice all the time. I read the papers on Friday, friend, and *you're* giving me advice. I listen to wcco and Howard Viken is giving me advice."

"And yet," I interjected, "there are people a man simply must trust. Traditionally, the bartender has functioned as a wailing wall, dartboard and some kind of sociological mop."

"Did you come here," Winters asked, "to interview me or sweep out? What I'm saying, those ratings just don't ring. Let's take a typical character needing advice. He don't have enough money. This is not only sad but universal. So he goes to the banker for advice. The banker tells him to take out a loan. He goes to a lawyer and one way or another he ends up signing something. He goes to a cop and he gets grilled, and he goes to a dentist and he gets drilled. If he asks a taxi cab driver he's probably gonna get the door slammed on his fingers.

"Now if he asks the bartender about money problems the bartender can go one of two ways. Personally, I would tell him either to take a part-time job or improve his sex life."

"Could he do both?" I asked.

"It is very doubtful," Winters said, "that he would have the time."

Paul the Sheik Changes Tents

Whatever your ignorance of professional football, you should join me today in rebuking the Minnesota Vikings for firing Paul Flatley, the noblest dude in town.

Disregard the fact that Mr. Flatley is a gifted football player, a commodity in short supply in the Viking organization over the years. You should be weeping today not for the Viking owners nor the Viking statisticians but rather for at least two hundred airline stewardae who made more passes at Flatley than the Viking quarterback.

Among the legendary boulavardiers in the heady world of fun and games during the past decade, the names of Green Bay's Paul Hornung and baseball's Bo Belinsky are supposed to lead all the rest.

"Don't believe it," a Northwest Airlines stewardess told me a few years ago. "And don't ever identify me as a Northwest Airlines stewardess, because the company worries about its image and would like everybody to believe its girls work in candy factories and read U. S. News and World Report on their hours off.

"The truth is, they never made another guy like Paul Flatley, which may be a bad figure of speech but which is the absolute truth. Alongside Flatley, Hornung and Belinsky were Hairless Joes in the vestibule and I do not speak from hearsay."

You should be quickly apprised that the lady's testimony reflects the early, formative period of the Messrs. Hornung and Flatley, both now irredeemably married and thus far removed from the temptation for further dalliance. About Belinsky my information is sketchy and usually comes to me now from the Police Gazette, the police blotter or Sid Hartman's mailing service.

Flatley ultimately was taken into custody by a young woman of flawless beauty, taste and trapline management who naturally brooks no foolishness. The occasion of their wedding plunged half of the town's bachelor girls into mourning and, I understand, so affected the Bloomington stewardess force that many of airborne nightingales have now renounced the profession and are living out their years meditatively and austerely as chaperones and clerks in the Out of Sight shop.

About his accomplishments in this field, Flatley maintained a calm, masculine restraint that he relaxed only at the Bemidji training camp for the benefit of his battery mate, quarterback Francis Tarkenton.

Tarkenton was a preacher's son, a conservative in social affairs and yet a man of buoyancy and good humor who enjoyed a good story. Flatley's accounts of his off-season hell-raising invariably left Tarkenton hysterically limp.

I have always contended that Tarkenton passed to Flatley not so much out of necessity as out of awe.

But Paulie is gone now, to return Saturday night in the uniform of the Atlanta Falcons, who acquired him 35 seconds after he became available on waivers. The teams play Saturday night, the Viking versus the Falcons. This is a contest, as the sporting authors say, where if the past records mean anything, the game simply would not be played, as a favor to both teams.

Despite some small familiarity with pro football, I cannot tell you why the Vikings released Paul Flatley, except to say this is part of the organization's masochistic pattern that began when it dry-gulched the best talent man in the business, Joe Thomas, and then allowed Tarkenton and Van Brocklin to cut off each other's heads simultaneously. There is considerable talent left, admittedly, but the big dimension characters and personalities are being effectively removed, leaving only Jim Marshall—and he hasn't picked up a fumble in years.

You should be aware that in his efforts to be fair and kind with Flatley, the head coach stumbled into a tangletown of logic that left us wondering whether the wrong guy was being released.

As I gather it, Flatley was excised because of some kind of crisis of confidence between the quarterback and the receiver—the problem being that the quarterback couldn't get the ball to the receiver. One of the reasons for this was that the quarterback wasn't *throwing* the ball to the receiver.

Now I think Bud meant to tell us Flatley wasn't able to maneuver into the open under Bud's system. The way it comes out, however, they are firing the horse because the jockey couldn't see straight.

"Putting it another way, Klobuchar," announced one of the news desk commandos, Ed Bolton, "we don't object to the way you handle your job but the copy boys just aren't able to get our memos to you lately because they are sitting there solving the world's problems, and so we are now going to correct this breakdown in communication by firing the author."

Pals, the man is kidding, I'm sure. I'm sure.

Tim Arrives, And We All Flutter

Despite decades of experience in natural disasters such as floods, blizzards and tornadoes, Upper Plainsmen were not quite sure of their ability to cope with still another — the arrival of Tiny Tim, the petuniaesque entertainer. Editor Lee Canning dispatched the writer in the first wave of resistance.

THIRD ROW OF FLOWER POTS, INTERNATIONAL AIRPORT — If Tiny Tim is authentic, the world is a lot closer to the petunia patch than we imagined.

By now you may have heard the entertainer showed up with his hair in ringlets, his ukelele in a department store shopping bag and his voice ecstatic with glee, which surprised many of us because the weather was gloomy and tended to dull some of the impact of his lavender socks.

"Is he going to sing in that outfit?" I asked one of the aides, referring to his floral tie, chalk-stripe gray shirt, baggy plaid pants and celestial blue jacket.

"He not only sings in it," the aide said, "he sleeps in it."

Canning, if you will forgive the figure, the flower of Twin Cities journalism was there and so I am at a loss to explain the line of questioning. With the Montreal Canadiens downtown drinking beer on their day off and the Twins' Billy Martin in this very airport, the authors insisted on consulting Tiny Tim on hockey, Zoilo Versalles and Mud Cat Grant.

The mention of Zoilo's name aroused something maternal in Tim's moist, love-filled eyes. His eyebrows swayed with the rhythm of the room's air conditioned currents and his nose swept painstakingly from left to right. It is a truly remarkable instrument, described as not only having the general shape of the state of Florida but the size.

Tim seemed to be saying that Zoilo might be restored not only as a soul creature but as a usable shortstop if somebody understood him. I confess, Canning, I did not take notes, being partially blinded by the radiance of Tim's upper plate.

Momentarily, I considered summoning the Twins' manager, who was boarding on another concourse. Martin used to understand Versalles, and might again. But the juxtaposition of those two stunning profiles, one made concave by plastic surgery and other convex, might be too much even for the sophisticated camera equipment in attendance.

During sentimental moments such as these, of course, I am sure we are viewing the genuine Tiny Tim, who puts powder on his face, he explains, for purity.

But the onlooker, gripped by a vague sense of uneasiness in this environment, begins searching around for familiar creatures with whom he may share his discomfort. I gravitated immediately to one of the beacons of television stability, wcco's Dick Stuck.

"Stuck," I said, "if he sings 'Tiptoe Through the Tulips' I'm going to head for the door."

"Don't you like falsettos?" he asked.

"Is he singing it or wearing it?" I replied.

But Tim sat there imperturable, flanked by one songwriter who wore a brilliant houndstooth jacket and another who wore immense rose-colored glasses, giving him the appearance of a pastel owl.

"Stuck," I said, "are we really that far out of it?"

"Friend," he said, "give the downtown fashion houses two more years and you'll be sitting with the guy who looks like an owl!"

Hoot-hoot, Canning, hoot.

With a Rope and a Hairpin

Until this late summer day—on the wind-raked precipices of the 13,766-foot Grand Teton mountain —Carol McCarty's most strenuous act in twenty years was a mile stroll to her supermarket at Rockford, Ill.

She was scared but unquenchably saucy. Her feet were blistered from a 10-mile drag through the boulders, shifting scree and high-angled trails of the Garnett Canyon, and her skin itched from the long-legged underwear she had to put on now at three in the morning.

But she was going to the top with her two teen-age sons if she had to go the last 2,000 feet on all fours.

She was forty-two, a chatty and inquisitive brunette, the wife of the assistant to the president of Rockford College. Two days earlier she had been introduced to rock climbing at Glen Exum's school of mountaineering and, impetuously, insisted that she and two of her four sons, Tom, 17, and Mike, 15, climb the highest peak in this pinnacled wilderness the very next day.

"It isn't like deciding at the last minute to go to the PTA meeting," her guide advised. "Anybody of reasonable stamina, balance and nerve can get to the top of the Grand, with help. But do you think you can stay up with the group?"

"It doesn't matter if I stay up," she announced briskly. "If I have to, I'll catch up."

I encountered the McCartys accidentally the next day at Exum's base cabin, where I asked about partners for my climb on the Grand. Exum handed me a rope and invited me to join the Illinois party, two others, and **Dean Moore,** a powerful young guide.

Whereupon the mountaineering veteran launched into the climbing version of the pre-game fight talk, lifting the novices toward the heights with the soft passion of his language and also scaring the hell out of them from time to time.

"If you do not punish yourself in one way or another on your first climb of the Grand," Exum said, "you are missing an emotional experience. You will get tired, but you should not give up. The human body is a remarkable instrument. I have climbed with an old man who was desperately fatigued, who came down from the mountain gasping, with his eyes swimming in the tears of exhaustion, but he made the climb."

Carol McCarty absorbed all this with large eyes and an open mouth. But she got onto the trail and, predictably, began falling behind after a couple of miles. I lagged to keep her company. She was wheezing but convivial, resorting now and then to the time-graced and gentle deception of admiring the wild flowers to grab a few more gulps of air.

Ahead her sons shook their heads in the fashion of tolerant young men viewing the dodderings of the elders, but they loved her and admired her immensely.

We rose at 3 a.m. the next day after spending the night in the sleeping bags of the quonset hut at the 11,500-foot saddle between the Grand and Middle Tetons. The moonlight washed this bouldered plateau where we stood viewing the Exum ridge that vaulted into the starry infinity above us.

For an hour and a half we climbed in darkness. The lady from Rockford roped immediately behind the guide, climbed unassisted most of the route, but did not object when Moore lent an agreeable tug on the rope on the more difficult pitches.

At 9 a.m. in bright sun and calm sky, we walked onto the summit. The lady did not seem tired now. She embraced her sons and divested herself of one of the routinely immortal summit quotations that is expected of every climber: "The girls back at the club ought to see me now."

And, on the way down, when the time came for the party to rappel or rope down a 120-foot vertical wall, the brave little lady came apart for one forgiveable moment.

On a rappel a climber literally walks down the wall, backward, or free-drops, using a double rope as a seat-sling and brake. Fifteen feet from the bottom Carol convinced herself she was out of rope, and began screaming her head off in the style of the typical housewife who has run out of Rinso White.

To which Tom responded, from the base of the wall, "Aw, Ma, quit your screeching and come on down."

Which she did, maternally.

A President Abdicates

Lyndon Johnson's announcement surely removes the final shred of sanity from the political year of 1968.

On all political oracles, who had the whole election figured out, it pinned the horns of ignominy — finally and permanently — and put them in the same bin with the rest of the blind guessers.

There was Lyndon Johnson on the wide screen, in an astonishing, unscripted valedictory, telling the nation he would not seek his party's renomination for the presidency and would not accept it if offered.

For this moment he made us part of history. It was a bewildering spasm. He stunned us because we had no warning. His entire character, his stubbornness, his ego, his pride, his Texas orneriness, left us unprepared for the sight of a tough president renouncing any further claim on the most powerful office on earth.

And yet, we might have had some suggestion of it, in the intimacy with which Johnson spoke to the public in the forty minutes that led up to his declaration.

He appeared to be a man who, in language, tone, and stage manner, was trying to achieve what the polls tell us he has never had — the affection and sympathy of a people he has led but not often inspired.

It is doubtful that he had ever been closer to the people than he was last night, or, probably, they to him. His statement on the American commitment in Vietnam had a sound of temperance and reasonableness without yielding any of the old Johnson tenacity.

It was hard to believe that Lyndon Johnson was being anything less than earnest when he spoke of the anguish of the office, of his wish to protect not only the American dream but the prestige of its dollar, the uncrossable lines of its militarists and yet somehow to try to satisfy the yearnings of the rising colonial nations.

One does not have to be a political cynic to appreciate that Johnson has been no political saint. He got into this fix because of an uncompromising will which some call ego. And one has to assume that another of greater personal buoyance and believability, whether merited or not, a Franklin Roosevelt, or Dwight Eisenhower or John F. Kennedy, might have found a way out without abdication.

To the typical American, the most admirable part about Lyndon Johnson in the last twelve months is that he has been his country's president, whether guided rightly or misguided on Vietnam, more than he has been its ranking politician.

All of which makes his decision of last night, to the viewer in his living room, all the more baffling. Finally, you have to get it down to pretty primitive language. Who would have imagined Lyndon Johnson walking away from a battle?

Unless he is acting on medical advice that gives him no choice, this seems to be what he is doing. You may or may not buy his logic when he tells you he doesn't want the presidency in this hour of the nation's history to get mixed into politics.

Roosevelt did, of course, and so did Lincoln. But Johnson finds himself conducting a maddening war that many people believe is wrong. It has divided the people, robbed the country's fighting men of the fundamental honor that should be accorded good soldiers, and, last night, wrung from the President himself the implicit admission that he does not know how to end it.

The country is left to speculate on what finally pushed Johnson to this extremity. Was he really fearful of being rejected at the polls, or that he could not function as a president and still fight a political fight within his party and against the other? Do his medical advisers know something we do not?

And so now, whither? There is almost too much congestion for one state to bear, the thought that we may have not two but three sons in the presidential hammerthrow — Eugene McCarthy, Harold Stassen and now Hubert Humphrey. There may still be time for Mrs. Butler.

Joe Namath Slays the Knights

There is an easy rhythm and ring to it, a sound of chivalry, as we link yet another new immortal today to the idols of our youth, Frank Merriwell, Sir Galahad, Tom Mix — and now Joe Namath.

I know there will be purists who argue that time has not yet confirmed Joe's right to enshrinement into this brotherhood of gallantry and good works. And that further, it is entirely possible that Joe would disrupt his investiture proceedings at the round table by claiming that he knows at least five knights who handle their lances better than Galahad and that Mix couldn't hold his liquor.

We may as well accept it. In 2½ hours of football Sunday, Joe dissolved the myths of centuries that had nurtured our simple faith in the ultimate triumph of virtue. At the very minimum, you grew up to expect virtue to get at least a tie, as symbolized by Ara Parseghian of Notre Dame two years ago and re-affirmed by Bud Grant a year ago.

But today, in the wash of Sunday's Super Bowl victory by the New York Jets over Baltimore and the National Football League, we have to take a hard look at all of our adolescent fantasies, swallow bravely and tell the kids of America:

"Well, at least he doesn't drink Scotch during the half, which ought to be a very good lesson to you on the benefits of sacrifice and self-discipline."

What we have here then is the prototype of a new vintage matinee hero, a Jack Armstrong on the rocks.

The fairy tales, my melancholy friends, are dead. The same thing would have happened if the sheriff outshot Robin Hood at the annual hole-in-one archery festival on the downs. Namath beating the Colts, tradition and Jimmy the Greek of Vegas, all in 2½ hours, is no less shattering to mankind's ongoing belief in justice-with-mercy than Perry Mason losing to Hamilton Berger.

How are you going to explain it to the kids? You might as well tell them that Bob Richards is a tobacco auctioneer on the side or that Vern Gagne wears falsie biceps.

The whole concept of the morality play in the movies, on television and on the playing field may have to be revised in the light of Joe's conquest on Sunday. The Dodge boys will switch to dark hats. Bud Wilkinson might have to go to snuff. You will have to take your 8-year-old aside for a manly dialogue and inform him quite frankly: "Percy, the ball game IS over before the final whistle, especially if they've got the 18th commercial still to put on and they're outa field goal range anyhow."

Now you may argue that Joe Namath is a roisterer, a loudmouth, a freako in styles, a vulgar conversationalist; that he accomplished the nearly-impossible in this special kind of endeavor by getting kicked off a Bear Bryant-coached team at Alabama; that he is a crass commercialist, an arrogant brawler and furthermore that he doesn't drink Beep.

All of these things Joe might modestly acknowledge. Unfortunately, he plays football rather well.

The trouble is, we are confused about how to cast Joe in the pro football version of the morality play. Until a few days ago Joe was the Menace. He offended the fair-minded men with his bragadaccio and he offended the women by suggesting that a female sportswriter was a bitch, a point on which the women might at least be willing to keep an open mind. We may now have to cast him as the Fu Manchu Prophet, the Quarterback from Manchuria.

Regrettably, Namath delivered. Despite all of our admiration for his skills and his defiance of convention, however, we have to concede that he could not have done it alone. The Colts, by carefully husbanding their resources, managed to save all of their atrocious football for the championship game. They played on a consistent and inspired level of ineptness that suggested that they could not have been that bad by themselves from start to finish — somebody must have been injecting them with boredom pills during timeouts.

An epoch is over, people. We were gulled by the brawny Colt linebacker who was so tough he was supposed to eat the panes out of the bus windows. Instead, we yield the seat of honor to Namath, who ran out of panes a long time ago and is now ready to start running over the pedestrians.

Send him a carton of Wheaties, Big G.

Flat Earthers, Stand Fast

Second only to the fortitude of the three astronauts themselves is the stubborn gallantry with which Britain's Flat Earth Society refuses to throw in its longitudes.

For days now reporters have been clamoring at the door of General Secretary Samuel Shenton. They have been requesting some kind of concession statement from the Flat Earth people, some hopeful sign that in the year 1968 humanity has achieved that breathtaking unanimity it has sought for centuries and now believes indisputably that the world is round.

Aware that at this intimate moment in history civilization is watching him, Mr. Shenton nevertheless holds up the cautionary hand of the bona fide scholar. "Do not," he says with measured calm, "rush us."

You have to understand the Flat Earth Society is not going to be stampeded just because three American rocketeers send back pictures in which the earth has the distinct appearance of a smudged beachball.

Confronted with this evidence, Mr. Shenton resolutely declined to flinch. "They said they could see South Africa and so on and on," he observed. "But struggle as much as I could, I couldn't see anything at all. If the earth is a planet, it would have to be traveling around the sun at more than a million miles an hour, and we never have had evidence that the earth is moving around the sun."

Whereupon the Flat Earth Society flung down the celestial gauntlet, stripped down to its Orion Belt and declared:

"Now if they show us a very clear picture which does not show all the continents and the edge of the picture is out of perspective, then that would prove the earth is round."

You might argue all it would prove is that Frank Borman can't read the light meter, like the rest of us. And yet there must in our hearts be some grudging admiration for this die-hard organization which still bravely waves its small flag, even though it does seem to be drooping below the horizon a bit where the curvature of the earth comes in there.

What they have in the society, you see, is stamina. The Flat Earth people and their forebears successfully resisted Magellan when his ship circumnavigated the earth. As a matter of fact you might recall that while the Flat Earth Society lived on in Britain, Magellan lost his head in the Philippines.

Succeeding generations battered the gates of the society's citadel. Wiley Post flew around the world in eight days. Howard Hughes did it in three. Mike Todd took 80 but made more money than Post.

Thousands have gone east by heading west — solo navigators, world travelers and freeway drivers. The Flat Earth Society insists that while they may be traveling in circles, they are really moving in a flat plane. They are, in effect, chasing themselves. I grant that on the freeway cloverleafs at least, this may not necessarily be mythology.

But one by one some of the most obstinately-held beliefs of the ancients have toppled. There was the theory about the great submerged continent of Atlantis, and how it would never reappear. Yet we see remnants of it at Elba and Weaver, the southeastern Minnesota hamlets which merge for a few days each June.

They said Columbus discovered America, but we know now it was actually discovered by the Alexandria, Minn.,

Chamber of Commerce, which kept the minutes of its early meetings on a Leif Erickson runestone.

Thus we see that man surrenders his most cherished convictions only under the harshest pressure, and is not always frightened by facts and certainly not by film. In the offices of the Flat Earth Society, for instance, they now admit taking another look at their theory but insist on maintaining some of their symbolic customs. The organization still operates the only delicatessen where they serve matzoh squares.

And so what are we to do with this most spectacular of lost causes, friends? Our first thoughts, of course, go with the astronauts and their wondrous adventure, and so must our sympathies. Despite a journey to the moon, no travelers have been granted less privacy. When one of them goes to the bathroom, 2½ billion people know about it.

It is entirely possible, I suppose, they are bringing earthward new and unimagined geological findings of their own to explode yet another ancient theory. You might visualize Lovell turning to Borman with the observation: "You know Frank, just under the rim of that crater, I would have sworn I saw a sign saying Target Clearance Sale."

Stay Young While Inverted

The opening of the European Health Spa's latest shrine to dietetic decadence in Brooklyn Center, brought to my office door an infuriated young woman in black leotards and agitated eyebrows.

"The Roman baths and chrome bikes are okay for women with narrow horizons and broad hips who need comfort," she said, "but if it's a deeper world you're looking for — spiritually, physically and psychologically — the answer is yoga."

With this the lady capsized on the spot, executed a spectacular turning movement and resumed the conversation standing on her head.

"My dear Mrs. Larson," I objected, "either I am going to have to assume the same posture in the interests of chivalry, or you will force me to address your ankles."

"Your preference," she said reasonably, her voice rising from the tile squares in a superb demonstration of breath control. "I can maintain this position for some time unaided, after which I might want to nudge of couple of toes against your doorknob."

I admit having been swayed before by crusading women who were opinionated, by others who were dedicated but never by a crusader who was inverted. Mrs. Joanne Larson, 23, housewife, mother of three and professional yoga instructor, fixed her eyes mystically on my knee hinges and asked if it was all right to relax.

"Lady, if you relax in that position," I observed, "you are going to knock out two windows and a coat rack."

Mrs. Larson thereupon resumed the upright stance and revealed a face of elfin sauciness, totally unexpected in one who has immersed herself in the wisdom of the ages while soaking the kids' diapers.

"The trouble with those fancy spas," she said, "is that the calisthenics don't do much for the women mentally. Most people don't use more than 10 percent of their mental power. They get their minds cluttered up, full of static, so that they can't put their thoughts in compartments and learn the simple beauty and power of self-control.

"Now when you combine this with the physical discipline of yoga postures, you open an entire new world of fulfillment. These positions, for example, work on the endocrine glands, which produce hormones, the secret to continued youth and physical activity. I fully expect to live to be 100 years old, staying vigorous sexually for decades and decades into the future."

I interrupted here to ask her about her husband's views on this enthralling prospect.

"From time to time I remind him that when he's at the age of 75, my yoga training and discipline will place me at a physical age not much past 35," she replied. "Sometimes this amuses him. Other times, after he has had a chance to consider it, he seems positively frightened.

"I get the impression sometimes that my husband, although a good man with a sense of humor, may not be entirely ready for the future."

Friends, I'm with the shapely guru's husband. Society expects a man to bring to the marriage alliance a certain amount of energy and ingenuity but it doesn't say one word about headstands and deep kneebends. In other words, you can be a dutiful husband from the bank deposit window to the kitchen sink but Mrs. Larson now wants to throw in the parallel bars.

"Not at all," she corrected. "This is the sort of exercising they do at the Spa in Edina. It's all right, except most of the women did not seem to have inner repose and struck me as though they should have been out playing hockey."

But we have Mrs. Larson's word for it, from one of the few women in town who can invert you and convert you at the same time. Yoga, she says, will turn the raving shrew into a velveted paragon of mellowness and agreeability. These saintly qualities she seeks to impart in classes at the YWCA and the Historical Society in Bloomington, and who can resist not only urging but forcing every shrew in the precincts to enroll.

With this Mrs. Larson presented me with a jar of Pava Natural Organic Yeast P-900 which, she explained, as a stimulant to ardor is better than Wheaties, wine or eggs Benedict.

It tastes awful, pals, but it may beat the parallel bars.

For the Kennedys, Drums Once More

With rage and sorrow today we must wonder whether each stride toward a new society in America brings us measureably closer to a return to the jungle.

And yet the agonizing part of the shooting of Sen. Robert F. Kennedy is the futility of trying to focus our anger and horror, our inability to know whom or what to blame.

We can only meet the world's condemnation with our own helplessness and bewilderment.

It does salve our national anguish to recite the familiar language of shock in the wake of political assassinations and attempted assassinations. Yes, it was a senseless act.

Yes, it stunned us. Yes, it was appalling. And yes, it taxes belief that this could happen in the United States.

"My God," demanded a dazed and incredulous John McCormick, the Massachusetts congressman, "What IS America?"

The question is no longer the funereal rhetoric of the professional politician. We have used the same language before, after John F. Kennedy, after Martin Luther King.

We will denounce fervently but aimlessly the mounting trend toward violence, the greater permissiveness of society that stirs the spirits of anarchy in the hearts of rebels, misfits and exhibitionists.

We will brood over the rising power of lawlessness in the nation, and how it goads a gunman to shoot down a vigorous young senator in the early flush of an important victory.

But in our stomach we know there is nothing much we really can do about it, and the moralizing and heartsick reaction to the Kennedy shooting can do little to prevent a recurrence.

Somehow we have spun into a terrible cycle of political murder which beggars reason and solution.

If a man with an addled mind wants to gun down another man he hates or fears, laws and speeches and security agents probably will not stop him forever. We may declare a moratorium on political debate, but this is a gesture. Ultimately we have to turn our deepest sympathies not to the illness of the country but to the tragedy of the Kennedys.

There is some timeless biblical quality to the saga of this family, so abundantly endowed with material wealth, grace, intellect and ambition and so repeatedly ravaged by violent and premature death — first young Joe Kennedy, who might have been a president, but who died in a plane crash; John F. Kennedy, slain at the zenith of his life, happiness and power; the premature death of his infants, and today Robert Kennedy.

Bobby has been the least understood, the least popular of the young Kennedys, the most unsettling to millions of people who were swayed by the charm and conviviality of his brother but who have looked on Robert with distrust and dislike.

But there are millions to whom he has been the future, the banner carrier of the disadvantaged and the once-scorned minorities. To others he has simply been a Kennedy, requiring no further classification.

But for all of these obstacles and his disturbing drive, he has never been a man to underestimate.

Kennedy ran the rapids and walked the trails and mounted the hills not for show but because of a recklessness and thrust that needs this type of expression whether he walked by himself or in a crowd.

Perhaps, as his biographers have said, he was more comfortable alone and with nature.

And it was in a crowd where he was shot.

Eva Deserves a Recount

What has happened to the old feudal spirit of gallantry, ladies and gentlemen, that we would allow the barons of amateur athletics to trample the flowering romance of the Polish runner, Eva Klobukowska?

I raise the question on the eve of February 29, the symbol of Leap Year, when traditionally the matrimonial aisles belong to the girls with swift feet and the quick hands.

It could scarcely have escaped your attention by now that Eva (a) is a sprinter who won an Olympic gold medal in the women's races in 1964 (b) flunked a chromosome skin test to establish her sex (c) is being shorn of her Olympic medal as a result and (d) is engaged to be married to a college student who, we are advised, "laughs at suggestions that she may not be all female."

Our befuddlement in this matter is now complete. Eva passed a visual test a couple of years ago and was certified as being demonstrably female.

Medical science, however, says she is not a female chromosomistically which I will admit, is a very formidable way not to be female. Her boyfriend, however, seems satisfied enough with the girl's story to marry her.

The question now is: Does the boyfriend know something that medical science doesn't?

"Not necessarily," my private doctor-consultant informed me yesterday when he was asked to clear up the dilemma. "On superficial examination, even when unclothed, a person may appear to be a woman without actually being one. There is something in her make-up which is not right genetically, which actually makes her not a woman nor a man but, for lack of a better term, a neutral."

"And in the game of love," I mused, "there is just no place for this kind of middle ground."

"Game or war," he acknowledged, "the neutral usually ends up isolated. In most cases, of course, she may live out a rather bland life without causing any international sensations. But in cases where a prominent athlete is involved, you are bound to have controversy.

"The test is relatively simple and generally considered to be foolproof." It involves the taking of scrapings from the inside of the mouth and examining these for chromosome count. The count will establish the sex of the subject."

I pondered this information sadly. Here we have one of the ranking athletes in women's track. The temptation is to call her an Amazon, but the Amazon suggests South America and Miss Klobukowska is Polish, and you would hardly want to call her a Vistula. But she did win her events fairly, in competition with women who may not have undergone chromosome tests themselves, and not all of whom have such ringing endorsements from their boy-friends.

"Tell me doctor," I said, "doesn't the boyfriends reaction count for something? I mean the language of the dispatch was that he 'laughs at suggestions she may not be all female'."

"I would not want to take refuge in the old aphorism that love is blind," the doctor replied, "but without knowing anything about the merits of the case, it might not be idle to suggest that the boyfriend himself ought to take a chromosome test."

"But the implications in this are monstrous," I replied. "What you are saying conceivably could undermine the confidence of every suitor in the world, producing this form of peevish dialogue in the privacy of a park bench in the moonlight: 'I know I can count on you now, but will it still be the same when they count the chromosomes?' "

"Medical science is hardly infallible," I objected to the doctor. "You've been chasing the common cold for generations and I find Vicks cough drops still the best remedy. Isn't it possible the tests were incomplete or in error on this woman?"

"Anything is possible," he admitted. "Theoretically, I suppose, something could have gone wrong and the lady not only might be married but actually become pregnant?"

"In which case what would happen?"

"What else? The Olympic people would return the medals."

Rubbish Crisis on Dow-Jones Plaza

The pulse of the world will miss a stroke this evening while the besieged brokers of Edina make a courageous new attempt to fight their way out of a trash crisis.

"Edina," declared the village manager tenaciously, "can stick it out. I think we have proved that. Our preference now, however, is to ship it out."

None of Edina's thousands of admirers will quarrel with that frankly stated aspiration. Our hearts go out anew to this community in distress. This is no hour for petty gloating by Edina's less-prosperous neighbors. Until now, the community has been spared full paralysis because of its unique geography, it being easier to store two months of garbage in the three-car garage than in a one-car garage plus wheel barrow.

The shortage of refuse haulers, however, has not been relieved appreciably since the village custodians sent out the first distress signal, through the customary device of hanging a red lantern in the deposit window of the Edina State Bank.

"The response so far," said the village manager, Warren Hyde, "has been heart-warming, particularly that of our good neighbor and sometimes-rival Bloomington. We have received some truly inspiring suggestions from there, including one that we should drop our requirement for air-conditioning on all garbage-hauling trucks.

"Well, I want to brand that notion for what it is right here and now, a fable and a myth that never got beyond the first reading in council.

"Despite the fact that we have the fourth highest per capita income in the nation we dump our trash one bundle at a time just like anybody else. Anyone who suggests that we don't just doesn't know the basic democratic impulses of this community — that when we are confronted by surplus in any form the natural urge is to spread it around a little.

"At the moment we happen to have a lot of garbage in Edina owing to the withdrawal from business of our largest collector. It's a crisis, but we have not flinched in these circumstances before. We will tackle it tonight as we have others, without panic, and Lord I hope we can find our way out of this lousy mess in time for image-renewal."

In these circumstances my good offices were sought as a friend of the council and intermediary with other segments of the Twin Cities community. Hyde, for example, knew of my friendship with northeast Minneapolis garbage executive Bob Roff. Roff is in the midst of a spectacular season and has just come off a December of unparalleled success, climaxed by his selection as Rubbish Hauler of the Year at the annual Refuse Removers Ball in Bloomington.

"We are willing," Roff said, "to sit down with anyone, anytime, and talk rubbish. Edina's trouble is no different than anybody else's except there may be a few more empty caviar bottles in there and fewer Artie's TV Dinner packages.

"The problem is weather and not enough help. We have offered higher wages but it's a worker's market and who wants to dump garbage when he can drive an ice cream truck?

"The public really has never understood our problems. What we need is sensitivity sessions. The politicians talk about letting contracts and about refuse problems but they don't consult US, as though we have to open the meeting by splitting a couple of bottles of Airwick.

"Now, I don't approve any more than you of the sight of a civic-minded matron having to unload by herself, at the Savage dump, last month's collection of boxes, Christmas trees and mortgage notices without having a chance to change from furs to snowmobile suit. And I know all about the car pool system and I want to commend the people there for an original and bouncy idea, a Cadillac caravan from 50th and France to the dump.

"But in the long run the people around here are going to have to put the stuff out on the curb for collection."

Thus we will have renewed fondness for the trashman's role in our ongoing society, symbolized by this exuberant ode from a customer, published in the refuse association bulletin:

" *'Twas the night after Christmas when all through the
    house,*
    not a creature was stirring, not even a mouse.
"The refuse was piled, and not with much care,
    in hopes that the trashman soon would be there.
"His eyes how they kindled, his dimples how merry,
    his cheeks were like roses, his nose like a cherry.
" *'Twas the sanitation man who is jolly and quick;*
    he comes every Wednesday—and just in time's nick."

There are only 338 days until Christmas, Edinans.

A Bear is a Bear

Despite the company's elaborate denials, it's becoming clear that the Hamm's bear is heading for that dark zoological twilight from which the good ones never return — the whooping crane, the dodo bird and Shep the Faithful Dog.

This suspicion was confirmed a few days' ago with the news of Hamm's switch in advertising agencies to the bear-shunning dudes of J. Walter Thompson Co. out east, where the only hints of lakes and sunset breezes come from the garbage piles on the Hudson River.

The displaced agents are the locally-based brainstormers of Campbell-Mithun. Campbell-Mithun is the Uncle Remus of the Hamm's menagerie, and the bear's creator, keeper and psychiatrist.

I am airing the controversy publicly today not necessarily as a Campbell-Mithun sympathizer but simply to appeal to Hamm's conscience and humanity. Shouldn't the bear be granted the dignity of a quick and honorable oblivion? Does he have to go out as a hot-air balloon in the Winter Carnival?

This sense of propriety, no doubt, lay behind Campbell-Mithun's highly emotional outburst Monday when it virtually accused the present eastern-based Hamm's management of being against bears and "all the little wild animals."

This set off the expected hysteria in the brewing company's offices in St. Paul. There, the suds-mixers are torn between their childlike loyalty to the payroll department of the parent Heublein Co. in Hartford, Conn., and their animal-loving neighbors at the Como Zoo. It was like being accused of poisoning the pandas' water.

At approximately 8:40 last night I received this desperate statement from the local Hamm's office, hastily scrawled in honey: "Personally," it said, "the management of Hamm's all love the bear. Our employes love him, our wholesalers love him, retailers love him and beer drinkers love him. You will continue to find the bear in our point-of-sale pieces, advertising specialty items and at major festivals. He recently appeared at the balloon races at White Bear Lake to prove that he still lives, HE LIVES!"

In other words, the bear is being farmed out from the big, fish-filled forests of television and will spend his declining years in the brambles of moldy municipal liquor joints, sitting lugubriously on a case half-filled with Hamm's.

Friends, they said there was no room for sentiment in the malt vats but I never really believed them. And I don't really know whether the bear sold any beer for Hamm's, but he came into our homes, you see, and he was immediately accepted into the domestic chaos as a kindred bungler. He was the Joe Kapp of television commercials, somebody with whom all viewers could instantly identify. As a matter of fact, he was somebody with whom Harmon Killebrew playing first base could instantly identify, and very often did.

But Heublein pushed Campbell-Mithun out of the wilderness and back into the brewery and told it to peddle Hamm's by telling the nation's beer-drinkers all about some miracle in the vats that made Hamm's smooth. The trouble is, you can identify with a blundering bear and an irritated raccoon, but how do you identify with a kettle of hops?

And so in three years the advertising Gepettos tried to

sell Hamm's as three different kinds of elixir. First they called it pure and sparkly from the unalgaed depths of Minnesota's northern lakes; then they called it smooth from the stainless steel kegs in St. Paul and, in between, they put on a think-young Hamm-it-up campaign apparently intended to get the product rolling at junior proms and Bluebird meetings.

None of this seems to have caused too much alarm, admittedly, among Hamm's local competitors. According to television figures, Grain Belt will have outsold Hamm's by 282,000 to 254,000 barrels in the metropolitan market in 1968.

Hamm's thus is going to strike out toward new horizons, leaving unclear the fate of the current brand symbol, a kind of integrated Pocahontas who seems to materialize out of Muskie Bay and flow entrancingly through the forest with a tray of Hamm's beer.

The idea here is that what was good enough for John Smith is good enough for you, buster. Personally, the girl has always struck me being almost too fragile and young. I keep wanting to ask her for her ID card. They tell me, however, she is twenty-seven and has three kids, which is the real reason — history to the contrary — why Sir Walter Raleigh lost his head.

All of which leaves us to inquire, ultimately, whither the Hamm's bear? Does he really belong to an eastern absentee keeper? Does he belong to the animal-lovers at Campbell-Mithun? Does he belong to the ages?

Or does he belong at third base for the Twins?

The Patient Prescribed Death

His hand trembled erratically as it held the telephone, not in fear but in the spasms of pain.

For five days he had groped through the sleepless near-delirium of his final struggle with a kidney disease that had doomed him years ago. He came home Tuesday night to his apartment at 3415 S. 17th Av. in Minneapolis from General Hospital seeking some fugitive relief for his wasting body and his demoralized mind.

His 24-year-old wife tried to help him into the bed he could not see, but he was unable to lie down. He tried to sit but the effort defeated him. And now he leaned against a wall, struck it weakly with his pale fist, and wept.

"It's time," Ron Frederickson told his wife, "to die."

The kidney machine at General might prolong it for him another three weeks or four. Perhaps two months? How could the condemned measure the reprieve conferred by a machine? The doctors couldn't, not with certainty. Ron Frederickson was supposed to die nearly a year ago from the complications of diabetes.

He held the telephone; deliberately and in full awareness, he cut the last strand of hope.

"I'm taking myself off the machine," he told the doctor. "I'm ready to die."

Wednesday, a day later, he signed a waiver removing himself from further treatment.

He will die in another ten days, possibly seven, possibly less. His mind is slowly yielding to the morphine with which doctors are trying to smother the pain of his last days.

By the gauges of today's society he was a born loser, a child born out of wedlock who grew into delinquency in south Minneapolis; from there he went to Red Wing training school for shoplifting. He was a wise guy as a kid and a young man, flippant and defiant, though intelligent. His first marriage broke quickly and he was fired from his first job with the Colwell Press.

But the company stayed with him and so did the tough-minded faith of his Red Wing counselors who saw good in this once-undisciplined boy who might easily have walked the road to the penitentiary, without breaking stride.

He remarried, moved up in the company, toward the $800 a month with which the books will close on Ron Frederickson some time in the next two weeks.

Three years ago at the age of thirty he began to feel pain in his ankles. A short time later he began receiving three-times-a-week treatments on the kidney machine. It became clear the diabetic condition was terminal. Frederickson understood this.

"Either you accept death by whimpering it out," he said, "or you try to keep going. I stayed with the treatments. But I lost the sight first of one eye and then the other. Glaucoma developed and they had to remove an eye. It should have been an easy operation but I got pneumonia. They brought me past that but I started to get seizures and during one of them I broke a couple of vertebrae.

"Tuesday night when I got home I just couldn't take it anymore. I could put up with the blindness and even the pain but the futility — I mean being inactive and with no chance to do anything — this is the worst of all.

"I tell you I'm not afraid of death. Do you know how I feel? I'm kind of excited. Some time ago I became what

I think is a real Christian. I now really believe this is just a beginning, a schooling. I suppose I could be melodramatic about these last days, but why? The doctors will take care of the pain. I'm prepared. I never built any fairy tale castles of hope. I knew I was going to die. When I signed the waiver I knew what kind of symbol that was, like signing your own certificate.

"Some people say I've had a life of rotten breaks, but you know it's been so good for me the last seven or eight years. My wife, Karen, has been wonderful and my friends. I regretted once we didn't have kids, but now I don't.

"The two things I do regret are what she's been through, all her depression because of this, and that I didn't find a way to God sooner. I'm not a religious fanatic. I do believe. If I'm wrong, what have I lost?"

He tried to be the good, accommodating host to his nurse at St. Barnabas Friday night, telling her it was all right to leave the food tray, and never mind if the food got cold.

He is a slight man of 130 pounds, with boyishly askew blond hair and a willingness to talk relentlessly of his life and how it was saved. He says he does not consider himself especially brave, nor unusual, in his eagerness to get on with it.

"But you know," he said, "it seemed like such a little thing, the thing that destroyed me.

"Goodnight," he told a friend. "I'll be seeing you."

—A week later, Ron Frederickson died.

A Fruitless Vigil for Bashful Burt

To the fluttery hearted housewives who left the airport early in near collapse and dangerously unfulfilled, I want to disclose that Burt Lancaster did arrive in town at the intimately suggestive hour of midnight.

I received the news in a telephone call at 12:20 a.m. from a Western Airlines stewardess named Leslie Cruwys, who deserves some kind of flub stub refund for devotion to duty despite an aggravated case of the emotional bends.

"Mr. Lancaster," she revealed, "was vaguely divine on the flight to Minneapolis from Los Angeles. He wore an impeccable outfit of light-colored slacks, a powder blue shirt, a blue jacket and a coat with a soft fur collar. He seemed to be cracking up over a book whose title ends in 'Complaint' but otherwise he was politely detached, with a manner and appearance I would tastefully describe as fantastic."

"My good girl," I interrupted, "you must be aware that Mr. Lancaster's inability to make Flight 506 arriving at 5:05 p.m. left hundreds of housewives demoralized and in a condition of near-riot. This is how we usually encounter them on Monday morning sales day on the Nicollet Mall, but it is bad for their husbands on Sunday night.

"What happened to Lancaster? We surmised he was either feeding the birds at Alcatraz or chickened out after hearing the WCCO snow depth report, the theory being, 'how do you win an Academy Award playing the role of a lover with frostbite?' "

"Worse handicaps," she observed, "have been overcome.

But it was worth the entire flight just to hear his French pronunciation when he ordered Cabernet Sauvignon wine with dinner. Is that a favorite here?"

"The favorites here, Miss Cruwys," I corrected, "are Muscatel and Manischewitz, which may not be of classic vintage but do have the virtue of igniting well in snow-mobile engines."

Grateful for the stewardess' report, I telephoned the home of one Mrs. Len Brod of the village of Minnetonka, who had been one of the ladies in waiting at the airport. It was a remarkable scene, a flashback to the old news-reel epics in front of Grauman's theater. The girls were there in regiments, not the vulgarly curious but the legiti-mately idolatrous. You got the impression they all wanted to try out for the roll in the surf in "From Here to Eternity."

When Lancaster's flight was late in arriving, they began searching about restively for targets of opportunity. Ac-cidentally, a couple of matrons thrust an autograph book in front of me. The movement was not lost on the impa-tient ladies. For an agonizing moment I was afraid of being mistaken for a movie star. At length one of the matrons interposed, "You DO look a little like Danny Thomas."

"Don't be silly," I replied, "I look horrible in a bur-noose."

For the envious males in the audience, there will be no low-grading of Lancaster from me. Burt remains one of my favorites, as well as that of the lads in Stillwater Prison. Lancaster appeared in so many convict movies in his early period that as a pin-up feature at the penitentiary he still outranks the cons' other high-echelon inspirations, Sophia Loren, Frank Nitti and Billy Martin.

I fell into conversation with Mrs. Brod, an engaging woman with two kids and an attorney husband. "What,"

I asked, "attracts you to Burt Lancaster?"

"To put it in words of one syllable," she said, "he is marvelous. A he-man with strength of character, the kind of personality that cuts through all of the unreality and gimmickry and sham of the latter-day idols and creates the impact where it counts and endures."

"And that is . . .?"

"Must I be specific?" she asked, annoyed.

I confess being privately delighted by the turnout for Lancaster, one of the stars in the film "Airport" being produced on location in one of the local snowdrifts. Burt outdrew Tiny Tim by at least 2 to 1, proving it is still theoretically possible for a man to be a star in 1969 without talking soprano.

And so they came off the 506, and the ladies looked fruitlessly for signs of Burt. Everybody who got off with good teeth and large nostrils was suspect. "Are you a fan of Burt Lancaster?" I asked an old acquaintance, Mrs. Sandy Cohn of St. Louis Park.

"What Lancaster?" she asked, "I'm here to meet my mother-in-law, and if she thought the house was a mob scene wait till she sees this."

Well, they all left disappointed and thus I called Mrs. Brod to convey the news at midnight. I was greeted by her husband, who suffered the afternoon tolerantly.

"Even if Lancaster was there," he said, "I wasn't worried. There was still a ramp and two baggage claims between them. I don't consider Lancaster a threat. The worst he did to me today was get the dishes piled up."

The Civic League Raids the Dugout

The dauntless forces of virtue have struck once more in the city of Bloomington, this time with an avengers' assault on rowdyism in the athletic arena and the dramatic theater.

If we read this landmark ordinance correctly, it means some of the noisier and more descriptive athletes are now subject not only to being fined by the league president but jailed by the City Council.

In short, culture buffs, all of us — spectators, gladiators and thespians — are going to be under surveillance by the gendarmes.

What the ordinance does is to give the Bloomington police the power to arrest anybody at an athletic contest show or amusement who is drunk, profane, vulgar, unruly or otherwise unsociable. While the intent of the fiercely upright lawmakers is entirely worthy, I'm sure you'll agree, the question is how do you enforce it without putting half of the Viking defensive platoon in the work house and most of the North Star bench under indictment.

If the law had been on the book three years ago the Dutchman would now be working on his 300th ball of yarn in the Stillwater twine shop. The only coach I have seen in eight years who could claim rhetorical immunity is Bud Grant, and even Grant is vulnerable to a charge of impersonating a city monument.

Clearly, the Bloomington Council imagines Metropolitan Stadium and Arena — once revered as the sanctuary for the free and the knave — as some sort of mutinous St.

Trinian's. Mayor Thomasberg is now going to wear the robes of headmaster, the Alistair Sim of Cedar Av.

The mayor's field commander, Police Chief Clarence Coster, is not quite sure how the ordinance got changed to include the participants as well as the spectators. He did not have time to theorize yesterday, however, having spent most of the day trying to recruit four French-speaking beat patrolmen for use when the Montreal Canadiens come in.

"I don't envy you, chief," I commiserated, "having to operate across international borders. Nobody in the National Hockey League ever heard of a game being postponed because the visitors refused to waive extradition. I have seen goalies in a slump but never on probation. If this ordinance is strictly enforced, the only way the hockey coach Wren Blair can come out for the second period is on a writ of habeas corpus.

"Mr. Coster, I raise these questions only because the Twins are about to open the home season with the triumphant arrival of that most rhetorical rogue of all. Billy Martin. Mr. Martin warmed up for his confrontation with your ordinance Monday by kicking the Sports Illustrated staff out of the Twins' clubhouse for all time, or at least until Griffith hears about it. When Martin hits stride, Mr. Coster, you may as well throw out the official scorer and hire a bailiff."

To all of these anxieties Mr. Coster held up a tolerantly judicious hand. "We have seen a number of player scuffles over the years at the Met," he observed, "and haven't made an assault arrest yet. Between you and me, the North Stars didn't make enough contact this season to arouse any suspicion of violence."

In the spirit of charity, I declined to convey this information to Blair, who already was convulsed in agony over the implications of the Council action. "I never urged our fans to be profane," he mourned, "just urged them to be loud, terroristic and loyal. There is no question they are the best behaved fans in the league. Now the mayor says he can hear vulgarity from the bench up there in the 16th row. Well, it's not so much the profanity as the proximity. In hockey, the fans are in close. In a theater now, the closer you are to the stage the more you are going to see the heroine's petticoats."

Without examining this provocative burst of wisdom too deeply, I had to sympathize with a situation wherein the Bloomington Council becomes the arbiter of taste and manners at the Met. I have heard tougher language in the bar at David Fongs than on the second deck of the stadium. What might be construed as erotic conduct in Fridley, on the other hand, is called a rubdown at Lee's Sauna in Bloomington.

"I hope they don't try to book the organist for incitement to riot," a North Star official brooded. "We may have to ask him to switch to 'O Promise Me'."

"The mayor ought to realize it's a very emotional game," Blair appealed. "What would the mayor say, for example, if somebody pounded him on the head and ground his nose in the ice?"

"I don't know," I admitted, "but whatever he said would take him 45 minutes."

Through all of the uncertainty, the Twins' Griffith remains the calmest voice of reason and moderation. "I see nothing wrong in trying to police the rough talk," he said. "There's just too damn much profanity in the outfield bleachers."

The Capital Gains Salesgirl

She looked temporarily brunette, with long lashes, a button nose, stubby contours, bell-bottom tangerine slacks and a commercial air.

She identified herself as a society call girl, with a marketing territory embracing Minneapolis, St. Paul, portions of Scott, Carver, McLeod counties and certain pockets of Koochiching.

Her ceiling price, she said, was $250 a night. This, while impressive, was described subsequently by at least one of her clients as a "somewhat inflated figure in terms of the Twin Cities market, from which you can subtract a hundred bucks or so to allow for normal feminine vanity."

It was hard to know whether this verdict constituted a cool business judgment, or was simply the morning-after reaction of a budget-minded sorehead. In any event, I was introduced to the young lady by one of the town's more resourceful magazine writers, the Twin Citian's Jeanne Blumenthal.

"I think," the author said, "Tessie would not object to being interviewed on the magic screen. She is frank about these things and considers herself a specialist in giving advice to Twin Cities' housewives on how to have a successful marriage."

Accordingly, I was admitted to the lady's suburban apartment, stylishly furnished, mobiled and carpeted in the fashion of a toney businesswoman of the times.

"The social arbiters tell me," I began, "that what you do for a living is not only immoral, but illegal."

"That is correct," she said, "but it is extremely profitable. The thing is, you have to think about status and style. I am very particular about the people I associate with."

"I take it, then, you prefer professional, cultured people."

"Bankers," she corrected, "are better, everything being equal."

The lady, it developed, is what one of my sportswriting colleagues would describe as a former native of Anoka. She married at a relatively early age and was divorced after a couple of years, when she acquired nomadic tendencies and expensive habits.

"And so," I observed, grasping the scenario, "after months of anguish and inner torment, with a sense of shame and profound fatalism, you entered into the life of a scarlet woman."

"Don't be silly," she said. "The decision wasn't that tough. The money is great. And the word, incidentally, is call girl. I make as much as $700 a week, wear finery, know rich people, listen to their troubles and generally have a ball."

I admit this last exposition smashed some of my operatic illusions. I had this image of the guilt-wracked courtesan caught between powerful forces of destiny, struggling to escape a web of sin if only the right chemistry asserted itself, or at least the right capital gains daddy from Bloomington.

"To be adult about it," she acknowledged, "I have no intention of getting into legitimate work, for the simple reason that this pays better than anything I can think of. Oh, I may retire after several more years and set up a little boutique shop, but right now I'm clearing in the neighborhood of $17,000 a year and really can't afford to be upright even if, as the expression goes, I were so inclined."

"Naturally, you cheat on your income taxes."

"Naturally, although I am wise enough to realize the government might get suspicious, so I report some of my money, listing myself as a seamstress."

"And thus it is clear," I concluded, "that somebody is getting well-basted, possibly the government and occasionally your customers."

"I operate on referrals," she said, "entertaining important people for important companies and, in addition, have a stable of regulars, most of whom are very fond of their wives but need more inventive sex lives. Personally, I don't drink, don't lie and consider myself morally superior to a lot of women who give it away and convince themselves they do it for love."

"And you are more moral because you take money for it," I said, puzzled by this quick turn of logic.

"Certainly. Now, what will we talk about before the cameras? I will wear a veil and show up at 6 p.m."

Well, I must relate sadly, she did not show, standing up not only me, but a young Baptist minister-counselor and a very inquisitive camera crew.

"So okay," she said over the phone, "I suppose you are going to threaten to give my name to the police and income tax people."

"No," I said. "You do disappoint the camera crew but in the process have scored a professional first. It is the first time they ever heard of a hustler with cold feet."

"This Was Your Pilot Speaking..."

Not since Jim Marshall seized a bounding football and charged majestically into the wrong end zone have we been graced with a navigational exploit to match the flight of Northwest Airlines' 716.

For the unfamiliar, this was the magnificent airship that soared from Minneapolis to Florida last Friday night, descended smoothly through the rain and clouds with electronic precision, and landed gracefully on the wrong airport.

True, it only missed Fort Lauderdale-Hollywood International by seven miles, a fractional figure alongside the vast distances the mighty 727 jet had flown. Nonetheless, it was an impressive performance for the 93 passengers aboard. This was especially true of native passengers expecting a leisurely roll-out down Lauderdale's comfy 8,000 foot runway, which now quite surprisingly had shrunk to 6,000 feet.

My first reaction on hearing the news was to deduce that this novel landing at an unmanned private field was not erroneous at all. I put it down as a first-rate piece of airmanship by an eager aviator trying out for chief pilot of Northwest's next peewee hockey charter to International Falls.

Later we were advised that Flight 716 was in truth aiming at Runway 9 Left at Lauderdale International but hit Runway 8 at Executive. As a sunny-weather flying novice, my fraternal sympathies go to the pilot, or the copilot or the baggage claims man, or whoever was at the controls.

Unaccountable things still happen in the blue beyond despite man's having mastered all of the secrets of the universe long ago. If you do not believe it, you should have accompanied me on my second solo cross-country flight in which I confidently aimed the sturdy little craft from Mankato to Redwood Falls, to the northwest. It was not until I made out the letters F-A-R-I-B-A-U-L-T on a strange hanger directly east that I realized I may have been getting misleading information from my gyrocompass.

And yet we deserve a little more illumination on this remarkable odyssey to Florida than we got from Northwest's department of strange flights. As I gather it, the official explanation is that the runways of both Lauderdale International and the satellite private field run east-west and therefore the plane's unheralded descent is easily understandable.

I conveyed this information to Roger R. Guerini, Plantation, Fla., one of the passengers, a man not only experienced in international flight but in the geography of Fort Lauderdale. "Migawd," Mr. Guerini responded, "I suppose we ought to thank all the saints that Highway I-95 wasn't running east-west too. We could have come down on the cloverleaf to Miami."

For a moment let us switch to frequency 118.7 of the air traffic control tower at Lauderdale and consult a Mr. Moore on events of this unusual evening. "We last heard from Northwest 716 when the pilot reported being five miles northwest of the field on his landing approach. When we didn't see him within a couple of minutes we got on the radio. After a small amount of confusion we learned he was on the field, which was fine except it just didn't happen to be our field."

"The aviators," I inquired, "now concluded they were

at Lauderdale Executive, the private field?"

"They thought," he said, "they were at Opalaka, which is the second airport south of us and the first one north of Miami.

"Anyhow, when the pilot seemed not quite sure of where the plane was sitting, our controller asked him to look out the window and see if he could spot a football stadium there, and he did, and we said sure enough he was at good ole Executive."

We will now shift frequencies back to Mr. Guerini, a horse trainer and plastic signs distributor. "The airline," I told him, "feels the mix-up may have occurred when a woman passenger became hysterical and the captain came back to soothe her shortly before landing."

"I do not know what she was before landing," he explained, "but there is no doubt she was hysterical after the landing. See, I live here. When we were coming in and I didn't see I-95, I said, 'lord, they got the wrong one.' Then I see the cement plant go by us underneath and I said 'they're gonna put it down on the beach, right on Pompano Beach.' But they come in on the runway and it was the damndest screeching of brakes you ever heard, and the hangars are coming at us 200 miles an hour, but the pilot did well to keep us in the ballpark.

"Then they announce they are having a little trouble with the authorities getting taxi clearance to the terminal, partly because there's nobody there. We sat for 40 minutes and brother, about this time I could have used one of these complimentary shots.

"But the guy I feel sorry for is the agent at Lauderdale International who may still be standing out there in the runway with his lantern waiting for 716 to come in."

The Day They Fixed the Foxes

It took the Christians 2,000 years to avenge their setback to the lions in the Coliseum, but we finally appear to have succeeded with Sunday's historic come-from-behind victory over the foxes at Eden Valley.

The town's Chamber of Commerce was modestly accepting accolades from all of the steel-nerved warriors today and offering the foxes a rematch in the wake of yesterday's thrilling triumph of the snowmobilers' art.

"It was a success beyond anything we expected," confided George Ruhland, one of the foxhunt's most energetic promoters. "We couldn't have done it without the foxes. I mean we needed something different to attract people.

"A lot of towns have snowmobile derbies. Putting the foxes in there did it. We did it to build Eden Valley, partly for the kids. To show how I really feel about animals, I put on this sign saying 'I'm a member of the Eden Valley Humane Society.'"

Touched, I asked Mr. Ruhland how long he had been a member.

"Actually, only a couple of days. We were getting a lot of pressure and heat, you understand, so we decided to organize a Humane Society Chapter. But let me tell you, a lot of people are sympathizing with the foxes, but we had no intention of killing any of them and didn't. You don't hear any sympathy for the young snowmobile rider who got thrown going cross country and wound up with a pretty bad cut."

I acknowledged our operative on the scene had not

checked the Brown's Lake field hospitals or the officer in charge of battlefield commissions and oak leaf clusters.

We didn't check the perimeter foxholes, either, because it seemed, well, inappropriate. "The truth is that the foxes never had it so good," Ruhland continued. "We spent weeks feeding them the best we could — chicken, other good things — and then all we did was ask them to do a little work Sunday. What's all the fuss? God made animals for men to enjoy, didn't he?"

You will concede this revelation has a certain amount of dramatic impact, the first formal announcement that the angels have now shifted from chariots to snowmobiles.

We have Ruhland's word for it that more than 5,000 people spent part of the day watching this elite of Minnesota's rubber-treaded Baron Richtofens bidding for glory and a couple of sawbucks chasing foxes in behalf of a new golden era for our children and our children's children. Spectators who got parched throats from the suspense had ready therapy in the form of a short snort of beer at the concession.

"The rules plainly stated," Ruhland observed, "that hitting a fox with the machine meant automatic disqualification for the driver."

"In this situation," I inquired, "did anybody consult the fox? I mean what's he supposed to be, grateful? Mr. Ruhland, if a man is after you with a cleaver and comes too close, what consolation is it to you if he loses his credit rating and you lose your head?"

"The foxes," he said stubbornly, "had plenty of room to maneuver in. But it was really something. I'd say we realized a couple of thousand dollars."

I think it is altogether fitting that a portion of this be diverted to the establishment of a Snowmobilers' Foxhunt Hall of Fame. In this the charter member undoubtedly will be the Twins' Bob Allison, for his soulful defense of mechanized fox-chasing in Sports Illustrated Magazine: "What are outdoor lovers and hunters to do in winters like this," Bobby Biceps asks, "Sit inside by the fire and look at television?"

The implication here is if you're bored either way, rev up the snowmobile and run down a fox. If I hit .247, Robert, I'd go out and hone a bat.

Graced by tons of free notoriety in the newspapers and on television, the promoters of snowmobile sideshows have been emboldened toward increasingly dazzling horizons and may yet make it to Coney Island. The Legislature is in a position to throw out some kind of straggling rear guard in defense of sanity but, as one explained, "foxes don't vote."

We may not have a technical violation of the law here, but we at least have a fresh burst of lunacy to confirm our suspicions that the hot-rodders among the snowmobilers will produce it when all others fail.

There is evidence of a new athletic hero emerging. "The fox they had in there today," he will tell the post-hunt interviewer, "he gave the crowd a charge, but he was a scrambler, and they don't win any trophies. The guys were up for this one. We had a picture of Reynard on the locker-room wall. We didn't mind he stole Al Jorgenson's chickens last year, it was what he did to Al's shrubs, like they were nuthin' but a water hydrant. You don't forget those things. So we stuck with the game plan and took home the bundle."

For your championship trophy, friends, send in your fox tops before the midnight deadline.

Waiting for the Bell

His nose ranges aimlessly across his face, shapeless as a garden pepper. It does not have much cartilage, but it does have character, a certain battered nobility.

This is the face of a fighter, a professional. He has the appearance of a man who has walked into a thousand walls. But while his face is pasty and scrambled, his eyes are alert, his speech cohesive and his manner courteous.

He is one of the few good white boxers left in the land, a 26-year-old onetime Marine from North Dakota named Andy Heilman, the fifth best middleweight fighter in the world. This is a largely moronic and sometimes crooked business, but Heilman is a good man of discipline and ambition.

He is sitting on a bench in the dressing room of the Minneapolis Auditorium an hour and a half before he is to fight a man named Tony Montano. For the last year or so he has been living in the never-never land of the professional fighter, where the money is lushly green and the women plentiful, if he wants them.

"The stuff will wear you out," he says of the women. "I stay away from it for at least ten days before the fight." His manager is bandaging his hands, and Heilman looks for a clock. "I been fighting for years," he says, "but it never matters who the guy is you're fighting. I hate the waiting. Guys come in and talk before the fight and I try to be polite, but I'm dyin' right now."

A door opens across the dressing room and a preliminary fighter, Mel Fields, walks in with an ironic and cordial smile. Fields is listed as being from Phoenix. He has just suffered a technical knockout at the hands of one of the locals, Rudy Rodriguez. The punch that floored him did not seem especially hostile or very accurate.

"What happened on that?" I asked him. "Well," he says, "my manager told me I'm gonna have a lot going against me fightin' a home-towner, and all, and so if I get a little dazed-like, there ain't any use going up against all of that the rest of the fight, so I should just stay dazed."

And so Mel looked suitably dazed until the referee stopped the fight.

Into Heilman's room walks a local fight personality and instructor, Ray Wells, a Negro. He confers on Heilman the ultimate respect in the fight trade, a colored man's salute to the fighting qualities of a white, in a sport the Negro now dominates to the point of monopoly. They talk casually and affectionately, without awkwardness, recalling their days in the Golden Gloves.

A door opens again and another loser walks in, affecting to be enraged by an official's decision that ended his fight in a technical knockout. "I had the man whipped," he says, "then I take this little awkward side-step, see, and the man hits me and I weave a little and the referee says that's enough to end it. I been fightin' since 1956 and nobody ever knocked me out."

He is a boxing gypsy from nowhere, heading back, and he has been paid $150 to come from Phoenix for this fight. The house attendant removes his gloves, consoles him and tells him what a good guy he's been, that he will win next time and exchanges the intimacies of one pal to another.

"By the way," the attendant says later, "what'd you say your name was?"

Heilman now is shadow boxing and snorting in his dressing room, and the cronies are gone. We can hear the sardonic howls from the auditorium where a good-natured and amiable boxing derelict named Ed Hurley of St. Paul is floundering through the ropes with another mediocrity named Al Banks. The ring clock registers it as the eighth round at the Auditorium but it look like Musetta's Waltz at the Opera.

Somebody yells " It's time," and Heilman walks into the ring. He is introduced as "The Dakota Kid," but the label is contrived and unnatural and the product of a press agent's B movie mentality. He is neither the Dakota Kid, nor the Oakland Kid, but Andy Heilman, a broken-nosed but civilized professional who now goes about the orderly business of flooring and beating the old man they matched against him.

It was a good match, but I would have sworn they laced the old man's water with tequilla or something stronger between rounds to keep him going.

Casey's Reluctant Courtship

Lovers of soapbox romance will lament the crude scenario in which Casey the Gorilla is forced to star as the amorous lead in a quadrangle involving two lady gorillas and a jittery veterinarian.

We can be grateful that the veterinarian, having accompanied Casey from the Como Park Zoo to Omaha, has now been dropped from the cast, thus removing a potentially complicating sub-plot from the script and leaving the audience free to dwell on the real poignancy of the drama.

You will grasp the conflict of the situation immediately, ladies and gentlemen. No suitor wants to go courting with fifty grams of tranquilizer in his butt. And yet this is exactly the condition in which the gorilla's Como Zoo keepers dispatched our bad-breathed friend to Nebraska in a flagrantly commercial venture to stock the St. Paul Zoo with more gorillas, irrespective of Casey's stand on planned parenthood.

I am speaking now for males of all description in the full realization that sometime in the misty future this kind of predicament might befall any of us. I know very few gorillas confidentially. And yet I am sure that Casey objects violently to the thought of embarking on a courtship in the humiliating posture of being dragged, under influence of drugs, to the boudoir of his chosen love(s).

"Under the conditions," I objected to my old confederate at the Como Park Zoo, John Fletcher, "how do you expect any kind of spontaneous ardor from Casey in his confrontation with the two lady gorillas in Omaha?

"At minimum," Fletcher disclosed, "we are hoping for a degree of romantic normalcy from Casey. Frankly, it is not always that way with gorillas. At Seattle, for example, there is a boy gorilla who is very fond of another boy gorilla, which is bad; in Milwaukee, there is a boy gorilla who is very fond of the zoo keeper, which is even worse.

"Not necessarily for the lady gorillas but for the zoo keeper," I surmised.

"That is correct, basically," Fletcher agreed. "Casey, on the other hand, seems rather standard in his drives, and we have every expectation of a happy culmination to his meeting with the blushing girl gorillas in Omaha, Bridgett and Benoit."

"Tell me," I said, "about Casey's first, tentative approaches to the girls in Omaha, now that he has overcome his early inhibitions."

"Well, our first readings of the situation are that Casey really seems to care. I don't mean that he is ultra-thoughtful in the sense of bringing bunches of chrysanthemums to the girls, but he does seem to have acquired a degree of finesse after his admittedly outrageous performance of the first few hours.

"I don't know whether you know, but Casey started out like a four-sport letterman at the senior prom, judging by accounts I get from Omaha. The chief veterinarian there tells me that the moment Casey was shown the girls' cage he rushed over with great hoopla, pounding his chest and brandishing his press clippings in the manner of a campus hero just named to The Minneapolis Star's **All-Metro** football team.

"And this tactic impressed the girls?" I asked.

"It bored the hell out of them," Fletcher disclosed.

His next gambit was to try to be intimately confidential,

in the classic style of a 546-pound Charles Boyer. You have to understand the setting. The gorillas occupy a rock-walled grotto in the Omaha zoo. There is a cage where the two ladies maintain a type of zoological duplex, each of them, I assume, performing the routine dusting and sweeping on alternate Wednesdays. Well, Casey sidled over to their cage from the vestibule of the grotto. From the testimony of witnesses I gather he dropped his voice in the fashion of the Parisian apache saying, "we will meet at the Casbah, cherie(s)."

"And what happened?"

"The glass door of the girl gorillas' cage is electrified. Casey was not only ignored but shocked."

"The situation," I confided, "has the sound of one of the chronic Friday night losers at Augie's Bar on Hennepin."

"The net result," Fletcher continued, "is that Casey is now re-deploying and may ultimately fall back on the tried and true formula of promising them anything but giving them Arpege. If I had anything to do with it I would give them Arrid. But the boy has persistence, they tell me, and may yet score."

"And the girls?"

"Their reaction is predictable. Bridgett was overheard telling the other, "he's not bad to look at, but what do you think of his style . . . the big gorilla."

The Shaggy Creature of the Klamath

For generations, legends about giant half-man, half-beast creatures have persisted in remote regions from the glaciers of the Himalayas to the rain forests of northern California. They have attracted hoax-peddlers but have also fascinated adventurers and anthropology experts. In April of 1968 they attracted a small, unauthorized and largely skeptical search party from Minneapolis.

The Circle A saloon in the lumberjack town of Willow Creek, Calif., enjoys a breezy local glamour as "The Purple Eye." It is so described because—as one of the resident tipplers explained—"that's the color you're likely to be if you drink too much and duck too late."

The customers drink frequently but, by pooling their strength, usually manage to make it out of the door by closing. For diversion they play dice, dance a bulldozer version of the frug—and talk about Bigfoot, if the stranger is inquisitive and the bourbon not too seriously diluted.

Clear-headed, only the most rash among the loggers profess to believe there is some huge, primeval wildman roaming the cloistered forests of northern California's coast ranges.

Nearer midnight, they will be less skeptical, when the old myths and grandma's tales of demons and big people are marbled into the amateur anthropology of the wilderness, scientific theories, commercial promotions and plain back-country blarney.

Is there an Abominable Snowman of the California

mountains, a real live capturable creature, an actual link between the ape and man?

"I don't necessarily believe the Bigfoot story, you understand," a plaid-shirted lumberjack said in the Purple Eye.

"But I'll tell you, where you guys are goin', when you're camped out alone, say two of you, and you can't get to sleep and the fire is dying out and you hear some noises not far off like a cougar screaming . . . Now, you really don't have to get scared. But you do say one thing when you hear that cougar scream, and that is, 'Luke, maybe it wouldn't be a bad idea to throw another log on that little old fire, and it don't hurt my feelin's none if it's a BIG log, Luke.' "

Seven people claim to have seen the creatures in those brooding Douglas fir forests. One, Roger Patterson of Yakima, Wash., a professional Bigfoot-chaser, claims to have filmed one in October. Patterson contended the creature was busty, seven feet tall and heavy-footed, presumably making her one of the larger floradora girls ever reported.

If the hairy Amazon depicted by Patterson's camera was the definitive wildwoman of all time, the photographer has been wrongly used by society and the scholars, because very few persons believed him—at the point in time when we moved our own corn belt expedition into the whitewater creeks and thick timber this month.

"What it might have been," a Willow Creek merchant conceded, "was some prankster logger or a bit player from Southern California dressed in a gorilla suit, and if you thought the old lady was ugly, you ought to see the old man."

It was either that, or Patterson was telling the truth and there really is a Bigfoot of the Siskiyou, the Western Hemisphere kin of the widely advertised but still-unauthenticated Abominable Snowman of the Himalaya, the Yeti.

Plausible?

Large and higher forms of animal have gone unreported for centuries. The blue bear of the Himalayan snowfields was not classified until recently and the largest gorilla itself not until the 20th century.

But a wildman, a half-human, half-animal, a 20th-century throwback to another eon, foraging undetected in the thousand-year-old firs and huckleberry thickets three hundred miles north of San Francisco—now there is a notion to tumble around in your imagination.

A good part of the tale, in California, in British Columbia, where the shaggy oaf is called "Sasquatch," and in the Himalaya, is demonstrable fraud. There is no dispute that some of the seventeen-inch footprint casts hawked around several years ago as Bigfoot tracks were planted by at least one Willow Creek gagster and probably more.

The Bigfoot legend, as a matter of fact, is merchandised briskly in Willow Creek in the same fashion that Bemidji hustles Paul Bunyan.

The operator of Wyatt's Motel, for example, maintains a padlocked iron cage wherein dwells a mocked-up monster, which assumedly is the worst possible kind of monster. A coin dropped in the box will set the creature grinding into action, moving its arms in menacing gestures.

On the edge of this tidy little lumbering town is a wood-carved rendering of Bigfoot.

More or less annually the shopkeepers gang up on the tourists with a Bigfoot Exposition. "Coincidentally," the town's weekly newspaper editor acknowledged, "we find more and more Bigfoot tracks suspiciously sprinkled around the logging roads the closer we get to Bigfoot days."

None of which, of course, is any objective proof that the witnesses who claim to have seen the creature are lying. Debunkers, believers and neutralists alike who explore for it agree there is no way on earth to prove the non-existence of the thing.

Cynics laughed at Jim Bridger's reports of steaming fountains in a place later called Yellowstone, and the early jungle sloggers in Africa were measured for the funny room when they talked about a race of seven-foot natives.

Is there a chance that the apostle of the apeman theory, author-zoologist Ivan Sanderson, is right when he theorizes that the Snowman might have crossed into North America from China and the Himalaya before the last ice wave and now have staked out a final refuge in the timbered wilderness of northern California, Oregon and British Columbia?

"As the old baseball man Dizzy Dean would have said," observed Como Zoo's John Fletcher, "there are two chances of that—slim and none."

Fletcher was the wildlife expert and portfolioed cynic in my party, a forty-eight-year-old native of the Washington state mountain country and an extraordinarily self-sufficient and curious man in the wilderness.

Against his prejudices in these things, he brought along a tranquilizer pistol, or capture gun, the idea being that we might be able to temporarily paralyze our quarry on the one-in-a-thousand chance that we would get close enough —assuming he exists—to lob an anesthetized needle at him.

"I make no such assumption," Fletcher said. "And even if it does exist I don't think we ought to be thinking about trying to bring it back.

"You know what would happen if we pinned one down. The first thing, every museum director in the world would come running here to try to claim the thing, bone him and stuff him and stand him in a box someplace in a corner."

The others, businessman-adventurer Monte Later of St. Anthony, Idaho, and the globular but quick-witted Minneapolis lawyer Jerry Singer, disbelieved the Snowman story but with less acidity than Fletcher.

I shared their disbelief, partly on grounds that if there really was a seven-foot giant of massive stride and strength, weighing five hundred pounds and yet furtive enough to escape entrapment, he surely would have gone on the first round of the National Football League draft.

And so we headed up the greening Hoopa Reservation valley toward the Bluff Creek canyon where, according to the reports, fables and gossip of decades, the big-footed snowman spends much of his time.

We paused to obtain a dispassionate estimate of the situation from Pritchard Jordan, the kingfish merchant of the town of Hoopa, a leathery, word-weighing man of caution and stability.

"For years and years they been talking about it around here," he said. "A lot of the merchants down in Willow Creek want to believe it because it's good for business.

"Well, that don't hurt anybody. I know where some of the tracks came from, and it wasn't from any apeman. Still, I don't claim to know all the answers. Indian kids around here years ago used to grow up being scared by stories about big goblins. Then again, maybe some of the tracks was made by bears, or something else."

Something else?

"I'll tell you about the country where you're goin'. Up beyond Lonesome Ridge out there up the Bluff Creek, once you get past the logging roads, it's the thickest, biggest wilderness you ever saw in this country. Like that forest ranger up there in Orleans will tell you, you can go for days and days without coming close to another soul.

"My friend, there are a lot of things in there that I don't suppose many of us have seen.

There is a hostile, desperate solemnity about the fir and alder jungle of the Bluff Creek forest.

When the loggers and stray miners leave, no man lives there.

This is a country for cougars, bear, bobcat and deer, of random mergansers fishing the unvisited streams. But even the wildlife is sparse, because only rarely does an alpine meadow interrupt the precipitous timbered slopes, and foraging animals know that the land to the south is more hospitable.

Anchored to the 60-degree slopes are great Douglas firs in thick congregation, fragile-trunked madrona trees with sheeny and elegant leaves, cedars, salal bush, alder, sword fern and wild raspberry.

The country should be beautiful but it is not. It is ravined and canyoned and it has high-angled forest bluffs, but it does not have the regality of mountained height. The government allows selective logging here, and thus the drainage canyons are a chaos of huge boulders, log snags created by timber-cutting and flooding, the galloping whitewater of the creeks and rivers, and perpendicular walls of rotting rock.

It has the power and profusion of big wilderness but lacks the warmth and order of the mountain forests more familiar to the western traveler.

I remembered a ranger telling us, "I don't believe there is a Bigfoot in there. But if there is one on this continent somewhere, this is where he would go when everything else fell to the road-builders and the real estate salesmen.

"You can go for a month without seeing anything civilized in there, if you know where you're going. If you don't know where you're going, you just are not going to see anything again, period."

This is the country where Indian kids grew up for centuries hearing jack-and-the-beanstalk tales about a terrible giant called Oh-Mo or Mettah who would devour them if they misbehaved. The fairy tale became part of tribal ritual, the monster dramatized in a bearskin dance around the campfire.

But it is also the country where footprints up to seventeen inches in length began appearing along the seldom-traveled logging roads more than a decade ago.

A couple of construction men reported finding a 55-gallon fuel drum weighing more than five hundred pounds smashed and flung into a ravine. Two workers told of seeing a man-shaped, hair-covered creature dawdling beside a logging road, and were, of course, nearly guffawed out of camp. Two doctors said they encountered the creature on a public highway near Willow Creek late at night.

Now this latter may be one of the more spectacular wee-hours alibis of all time, but it stirred the guessing game afresh in the logging camps and the little main streets of the isolated lumbering towns.

It brought a professional Abominable Snowman hunter named Pete Byrne into the quest, his bush-probing financed for more than a year by a multimillionaire from Texas, the late Tom Slick. Competition developed, casts of tracks were produced, and a half-dozen safaris were mounted for 1968, led by ours.

Before heading into the forest up the Bluff Creek road we interrogated the Bigfoot-promoters of Willow Creek, the merchants who are not quite sure in their own minds how much of this is believable and how much of it is merely profitable.

"Tell me why we should not regard the whole thing as a phony," I asked Bob McLellan, the manager of the town's Pacific Gas and Electric office.

"Well, the way some of the tracks are distributed, mostly. Yes, there were some fakes. But there are a lot of them that seem absolutely real, like the ones in the cast down at Al Hodgson's variety store.

"There have been tracks, for instance, found in places no hoaxster would ever go into, 17½ inches long, five inches wide across the ball of the foot, and appearing in series that indicated a 54-inch stride. How would you like to have that baby competing with you for a seat on the bus?

"I would simply have him pick up the bus," I said, "and spare us all a lot of trouble."

"The thing is that a lot of these tracks show minute changes in indentation, depending on the terrain. In other words, where the tracks go up hill, you find more pressure on the front of the foot, a delineation of the toes, a shortening of stride. It isn't as though somebody just came in there and planked a bunch of fake prints down helter-skelter.

"And about that, if the Chamber of Commerce bunch in this town was really scattering prints around the back country, how long do you think we're going to keep the thing secret from the rest of the townspeople, who don't care about the Bigfoot one way or another?"

"And do you people really buy the authenticity of the pictures taken by Roger Patterson, the ones showing the seven-foot, hypermammary Snowgirl shuffling down the trail?"

McLellan shrugged. "Who's to say?"

One who did was Syl McCoy, a locally-based forest ranger, an earnest, strong and likeable man. "I saw Patterson when he came out of the woods that night," McCoy said. "I never seen a man so excited when he told me 'I saw it, I saw it'."

No doubt Patterson saw something and filmed something. Sleuths have sought to pin down whether a large gorilla suit was checked out of a California theater supply shed sometime last fall, but nothing so far has been adduced.

And so we stuffed provisions for a week into our packs, strapped in a couple of tents and a sleeping bag for each, and slogged eight miles into the wilderness beyond the point where a landslide and crevasse made further auto traffic impossible along the Bluff Creek logging road.

We arrived at an unused loggers' campsite at near twilight on a Sunday afternoon. The recklessly bounding creek, white and emerald, poured down the canyon a few yards away and an 800-foot fir slope angled up to a high ridge behind it.

Our plan was to track the drainage creeks and the fringe wilderness of the crude roads, where nobody logged right now. It was useless to charge the steep, slick forest slopes, which wouldn't have appealed to a Snowman anymore than they appealed to a lawyer from St. Louis Park. In any case, no tracks were likely to be discernible there among the matted leaves.

For food we leaned on dry cereals, prepared soups, three or four rolls of salami for meat, rye crackers, dried apricots and raisins, a small amount of chocolate and a prudent portion of brandy and Canadian Club for a civilized warming additive against the 30-degree evenings.

Our private odds system took us to these off-the-cuff conclusions. There was a one-in-a-hundred chance that the thing exists in some aboriginal form close to the folklore conception and that we had a one-in-a-hundred chance of seeing him and a one-in-500 chance of capturing him.

A 20-foot steel cage being cumbersome to pack in, we settled for a nylon climbing rope, a short-range tranquilizer pistol of a type used in zoos, and friendly smiles.

"The only way we're going to get this thing back to Minneapolis is with an injunction," we were advised by the party's legal genius, Gerald Singer.

"Just one question, Singer," Fletcher observed. "Who's gonna serve it?"

Singer, with a child's fondness for cap pistols, strapped a .38 sidearm to his waist, giving him the appearance of a droopy-holstered wrangler from the Lincoln Del.

"There's nothing in this woods you're gonna scare with that thing," Fletcher said knowledgeably, "except the guy next to you in the tent."

I clucked at this but turned suddenly unhappy on reflection that I was the guy next to Singer in the two-man tent.

"I think we will ask you to check your guns at the nearest stump over there," I advised him as we headed up the trail toward Onion Lake the next morning. We split into two-man teams, Fletcher tracking with Monte Later, the Idahoan.

For five hours Singer and I trudged the lonely dirt roads and sidewoods uneventfully. The lack of any fresh boot marks suggested no one had been there all winter. Near Laird Meadow, Singer stopped and stood, pointing to a large, vague, inexact set of tracks close to a culvert.

"They're big," he said, "but I suppose they could be our own tracks from the morning, distorted by the mud."

"They could," I agreed, "except for one thing. We were headed south this morning. The tracks you're looking at head north."

Singer, my tracking sidekick for today, viewed the grotesque, footlike depression in the mud with a mingling of skepticism and alarm.

He has a penetrating intellect and a gushing, bon vivant disposition, but he is a son of the city's asphalt and mysteries in the forest unsettle him.

"One of two things," he said, "either I'm imagining that this track and the ones there in the mud around the culvert were made by a big animal, or they really were, and if the second is correct, tell me what I'm doing on this lonely logging road without another soul around?"

We examined the evidence up close, but there was not enough definition in the track to bring us to any kind of working hypothesis. We were intrigued by the recollection that this was the specific site, on the road to Onion Lake, where hundreds of Bigfoot tracks had been reported some time ago.

"One thing about it," I noted, "if it's really a track it's no forgery, I mean something planted recently by Bigfoot promoters in that little town.

"If they were going to play games, they would have done a better job than this. You can see where toes are supposed to be, but the only thing you can tell from this is that whatever made it has got terribly flat feet, and pretty big ones, because the track you're looking at is a foot and a half long."

However unclear, it was impossible to view the imprint in the mud, and the even less distinct prints around the culvert, without momentarily conjuring an image of some shaggy, furtive zoological freak, doomed by the accidents of evolution to rove the dark forests, evading the reach of man.

The stories of man's alleged encounters with the Bigfoot in California, the Sasquatch in British Columbia and the Yeti in the Himalayas are generally tenuous and largely unbelievable. There was one account from the 1900s in which a man claimed to have been kidnaped by one of the beasts and held captive by a Sasquatch family for six days.

His theory was that he was abducted for the primary purpose of functioning as a mate for one of the Sasquatch clan's spinster daughters. This, if true, undoubtedly would have made the abductee the most flabbergasted suitor of all time.

Mercifully, according to the account, he was released after six days presumably judged to be inadequate for the task.

In the same British Columbia territory, an apelike sub-human, about five feet tall, was supposed to have been captured in the late 1800s and sent to London for examination. It was never heard from again and conceivably could have wound up in a Peter Lorre movie.

And yet for all of the fantasy, undoubtedly many of the tracks in the Himalayas, at least, are authentic and so are some of the sightings. The question is: What made the tracks, an apelike humanoid, or, more probably, a bear or monkey-like languar.

This does not immediately dismiss the Snowman theory. But it was not until an English journalist made the provocative translation of the native name and called it "abominable snowman" that outsiders really got interested.

Have there really been "giants of the earth," goliaths of antiquity, the forebears of a creature who just might have made the tracks we were looking at now?

The anthropologist, Bernard Heuvelmans, is convinced there were, citing the discovery of gigantic jawbones and teeth in Asia that point to the existence of some kind of apeman ten to twelve feet tall.

"It is easy to see," he wrote, "how if a line of apes evolved in increasing size they would very soon have to give up living in trees. The mountains would be an ideal habitat, and there the snow would encourage them to become bipeds. Thus, in theory at least, a race of giant apes with primitive plantigrade feet and a tendency to stand on their hind legs could have arisen in the mountain snows.

"So in the end, had we not better humbly accept the evidence of those who describe the snowman as a giant ape, a sort of hairy ogre? Most people may reply that giants have never existed. But this . . . is not true."

And could they then have migrated to North America over the Siberian land bridge?

All very stimulating but totally, of course, unsubstantiated. In the few days we had spent in the prime Bigfoot country, we had only these crude fuzzily-outlined couple of tracks to go on, not enough at this point, really, even to make a plaster cast.

John Fletcher and Monte Later, meanwhile, had covered seventeen miles patrolling a road along the Lonesome Ridge about which some folk legends existed, wading in and out of the tributary Scorpion Creek to examine the soft shoreline that offered the most promising ground for tracking.

"There are these local tales," Later recalled, "about there being no life high up there. The implication is that this is the heart of the Bigfoot country, and there is something about it that repels and frightens the wildlife in the territory, as though it were some invisible barrier.

"Also, I talked to an Indian woman back at the Purple Eye who told about old tribal tales to the effect that berry pickers moving up Lonesome Ridge used to holler as they went, and when they heard something holler back, that was as far as you went, brother, because nobody ever wanted to see what was hollering back."

"I know," I observed. "You get the same kind of standoff on the last hole of Meadowbrook golf course."

"Well, what I wanted to say was that we saw plenty of

bluejays up on Lonesome Ridge, for all of the old super-
stitions, plus some bear and deer track right up to the edge
of the ridge there.

"But not really on the ridge."

"The only way you could get up on that wild ridge is
with suction cups and wire cutters."

We sat beside the campfire, a fragile flicker in the in-
scrutable sweep of the giant forest, and hazed Singer's
greenhorn newness to the wilderness.

"Big deal, you guys," he said, "the only thing we find
to hang anything on so far, and it's the investigating attorney from downtown who finds it.

"But I'll tell you one thing. If six weeks ago some fortune teller would have told me I'd be sitting here on a huge,
fallen Douglas fir in the middle of a wild woods, at the end
of sixteen miles of slogging, in water boots, with raisins and
dry oatmeal to eat, chasing the Abominable Snowman, I
would not have really cross-examined her. I would have
sued her for fraud."

Later turned to Fletcher, the party's resident agnostic
on the subject of the snowman, and asked about the tracks.

"It isn't exactly something you would pin on a church
door and reform anthropology with," he observed.

"There's this about those plaster casts back at Willow
Creek: Unless the track was fabricated, it was made by
something enormous, with fallen arches at that. And judging by the description of the tracks seen in series, they
couldn't have been made by a bear, because there's no bear
I know of that would have a stride four-feet long.

"And I never heard of any kind of ape in North America
besides the ones in the zoos. Also, if you use human dimensions as a guide, that is, comparing a human's stride with
the length of his leg, you have to conclude whatever made
this series of tracks had the highest inseam you ever heard

of, like about five feet.

"Now having tramped around in the western woods a long time, it doesn't surprise me to hear that whatever's doing it out here has flat feet.

"One thing notable about the cast is that there seems to be a second joint print made in the area of the big toe, of a kind you don't see made by a human toe. And of course, it just doesn't look like a bear print and is too big in any case.

"And so," he said, "if you believe the stories and film and tracks, if there is something in here, it's humanoid rather than anthropoid, meaning it's just about a human being. But we haven't seen anything or heard anything out here yet that makes you do too much speculation."

Monte Later, silent during much of the conversation, now interrupted.

"There was something, John," he said, "in the ravine."

A week in the silent and alien wilderness may coax a man's senses to the fringe of fantasy, but it cannot deceive him about the crack of a tree limb fifty feet away.

Monte Later is an experienced outdoorsman from the mountain trout-fishing country of St. Anthony, Idaho, a climber, skier, photographer and amateur botanist whose fondness for the big woods of the West is deep but controlled and his merchant's mentality carefully ordered.

He has seen and hunted the big game of the West much of his adult life—elk, deer, bear, mountain lion.

"There are two things I haven't seen out here," he observed with a sense of disclosure on the eve of our departure for the Bluff Creek forest, "a purple cow and a Bigfoot, and I never hope nor expect to see either one, although if I were a betting man I would pin my money on the purple cow as offering our best chances."

But now he sat before our campfire, poking the burning wood with a yew stick, and talking with a trace of awkwardness.

"I suppose," he said, "I ought to keep my mouth shut because this is how people get reputations, and the last thing I want to be is some kind of Baron Munchausen of St. Anthony."

"You have delivered yourself of what the lads in my trade call a disclaimer," I said, "and I suppose you are going to tell us you saw something on that hike you took up the Bluff Creek ravines that you cannot explain."

"Yes," Later said, and he was not smiling, "that is what I'm going to tell you."

Fletcher, the certified skeptic in the foursome, eased another wood chunk into the fire and edged forward to listen with tolerable interest.

"I didn't say it was an Abominable Snowman," Later said.

"I can't even say it was a bear. I know it wasn't a deer or cougar, because it seemed to be too big and dark for that."

"Well, what do you think it was?" I asked with what I intended as an affectionate cuff of condescension.

"I honestly don't know," my climbing partner said, balancing his attitude rather delicately between embarrassment and annoyance. "But I'll tell you what happened.

"It was about 2:30 in the afternoon not far from where that big landslide has torn away a couple hundred feet of the old logging road. There are hanging ravines below there where the woods slant down to the creek."

The site was familiar. The aldered and huckleberried gulches, carved by spring floods from the snowfields above and disarrayed by the tangled foliage of wilderness, lie in almost permanent shadow. In a ravine, Singer and I had spent ten minutes staring at the exact spot where we knew a deer to be standing—without being able to make it out.

"I was walking not far above the creek," Later continued, "and there was the crack of a limb breaking down in the ravine about fifty feet away. I looked down and saw the branches of a bush moving, and then I saw a large, dark form moving in the cedar and alder.

"In a couple of seconds it was gone behind the wild thicket.

"In Idaho, if the circumstances would have been the same and that's all I saw, I would have said 'bear,' and let it go at that.

"To tell you the truth, I had forgotten about the Abominable Snowman right then, and was really thinking about how good it would be to rest my feet.

"There were two things that got me moving.

"First, I remembered we hadn't seen bear in this country, although I know there are some in there.

"Second, the thing I saw had some height, I thought. I've seen bear on hind legs, but not often. You don't see them that way in the woods often.

"All I saw was this big, dark form, for just a moment.

"So I went down there, and I could hear something moving away in the brush, and suddenly I got excited and I was really moving, but I didn't hear anything else.

"I looked in the thicket where I had seen the form, and the underbrush was broken a little, all right, but the leaves were so thick and matted in there I had no way of making out a track.

"I moved a little deeper into the woods. And then I remembered, 'Okay, what if it's something that might come at you if you surprised it?' because I didn't know what to think, and I'm in there alone in the bush without protection. So I went back up on the logging road, although I did take another look around for about five minutes."

Later stirred the fire idly.

"That's a helluvan oration for something that probably doesn't amount to much," he said.

"A bear?" I asked.

"Probably," he said.

"Would you bet on it?"

"No," he said.

"Are you saying it was Bigfoot, Monte?" another teased gently.

"No," he said.

"But, I didn't say it couldn't be, either. Every time the experts and the ultimate dispensers of truth convince us they have all the answers, somebody digs a little deeper or somebody runs a little further and all of a sudden all of the experts are a little more humble, because we really don't know all of the answers of the universe, do we, or even most of them?"

Fletcher walked over to me with a mess kit full of cake.

"For your birthday," he explained. "We'd have asked one of the radio announcers to play a tune in your honor if we thought you were on speaking terms."

There was a tall, dime-store candle in the middle of the concoction, and it was clear the boys had wrought some small culinary miracle in the wilderness. Using a small sack of Bisquick, dried eggs, non-fat dried milk, water and five slugs of brandy, Jerry Singer baked a cake in the fireplace, using a reflecting oven fashioned by Fletcher from a rusty piece of Diesel hood discarded in the old logging camp. For frosting Singer used Whip n' Chill mixed with dried milk, brandy and water, cooled under a madrona tree. I blew out

the candle and drank the cake, the only 80-proof cake I
ever had.

J ohn Fletcher reassembled our Buck Rog-
erish tranquilizer pistol or capture gun for the last time
and filled the needled capsule with an anesthetizing drug.
"Maybe," I suggested, "we ought to do a little target
practicing with that thing before we head for Laird Meadow."

Fletcher complied. He handled the task with elaborate
detail and meticulousness, like a Guthrie actor trying out
for a gunfighter role in a Pat Buttram movie.

"I don't think we're gonna bring back the Snowman
with this glorified hemstitcher," he said. "As a matter of
fact, I'm a little worried that he might throw the needles
back."

Nevertheless, Fletcher loaded the pistol and fired in the
general direction of a huge cedar tree 25 feet away. He
hit an aspen.

"Were you aiming for the cedar," I asked, "or the forest?"

"If we get 25 feet from the Snowman up there on Laird
Meadow," he replied, "the only thing I'm going to throw
at the Snowman is a very friendly greeting."

Among the Bigfoot believers (and there are an un-
expectedly large number of them among the supposedly
blunt-talking lumberjacks of the territory) the creature's
timidity is proverbial.

"Two of the things we have been told about his habits,"
Fletcher said, "is that he is extremely shy and has a relatively offensive or abominable odor. Under the circumstances, you can't blame the thing for wanting to stay down-

wind."

We smiled charitably at this speech, accustomed now to Fletcher's zookeeper irony. For a 48-year-old man he had waded and slogged and bouldered and log-rolled with exceptional endurance and a certain amount of gymnastic finesse.

You needed this to explore the Bluff Creek drainage. In the search for tracks in this inhospitable country, where the timber slopes are steeper than the Matterhorn the only sensible course is to thread the creekbanks and the neighboring woods. Any Bigfoot with near-human senses would travel exactly as a human being would to cover ground here, and that is to stay with the lowlands.

For miles and days we had followed the Bluff, Notice, Scorpion and East Bluff streams, a wasteland of nature, dramatic but unlovely, a maelstrom of cascades, windfall, foliage-curtained forests and the rotting remnants of giant timber left by streamside loggers.

To make progress here one must walk or vault or dodge the fallen logs; or outflank the windfall snags along thin routes among the crumbling canyon walls; trudge a mud-shore or, when all other avenues are closed, muscle through the cold green rapids.

Not much of it is very dignified going and none of it heroic. Three miles south of camp along the Bluff Creek, Monte Later and I decided to turn east up one of the forks. We looked for one of the log causeways but, finding one, turned back to the river, 100 feet wide here and impetuously racy.

"There is no way," Later said, "except to walk across."

"How deep, would you guess?"

"I'd say about 3½ feet, leader old friend."

I regarded the sunshine of the mainstream shore to the south and replied, somewhat unhappily, "Okay, let's get our feet wet."

"At 3½ feet, friend," Later said, "that is not all that's going to get wet."

"Like you mean hips, also?"

"That is the polite form, yes."

We locked arms against the pull of the current and went in, up to the ribs. We came back four hours later, the same way, and trackless.

For two hours now we walked leisurely up the Onion Lake road to the Laird Meadow plateau where Jerry Singer had noticed a couple of big undefined tracks early in the week. The melting snowfields on the 4,500-foot hills sent rivulets chasing down the muddy trail.

There were tracks here, all right, deer tracks, cougar tracks, perhaps a coyote track—and three hundred yards above the switchback where Singer spotted the track, we found another trail of prints.

Large prints.

Again, they were old, perhaps months old, but they described a route that carried in the same direction of the earlier sightings, and this time they seemed to form a series.

"How far apart were the alleged Bigfoot tracks when the hairy one was supposed to be in full stride?" I asked Later.

"Somebody said 51 or 54 inches," he said.

"How far apart would you guess those indentations are in the mud?"

"I'd guess about four feet."

There was nothing remarkable about the prints aside from their stubborn insistence on being approximately four feet apart for nearly fifty yards of the road shoulder.

They were too old to bear any definition of the toes, assuming that whatever made them actually had toes.

Although interesting to the eyeball, undoubtedly they would disclose little to the camera. The film, in fact, almost certainly would require some artwork to indicate any patterned indentation at all. It was, therefore, no real evidence of anything.

"But there's this," Later said: "When you follow this crude trail for a while, you can start predicting where the next imprint will be. And that's where it it."

"So what we have," I observed, "is a series of rather untranslatable mud hieroglyphics which could have been made by an animal, or by some odd coincidence of the elements and the mud, or by something we don't know about."

"The other possibility," observed the deadpan zookeeper, Fletcher, "is Seventh-Day imagination, which I admit I am as susceptible to as the next guy.

"I want to congratulate you on not being bowled over by these tracks," he continued, "and I'll make the concession that something probably made them. I don't know what made them. All we know is that there appears to be a series of marks about a foot and a half long running down the side of the road. They are too indistinct to support any detailed examination or theorization. Maybe that's good. If they were precise prints I would move from being skeptical to being downright suspicious."

Later and I tarried for a while, looking down the road. And for both of us, I think, it was hard to resist the temptation to look over our shoulders.

We continued to Onion Lake another hour up the trail, past a chrome-miner's summer shack and into the snowfields. The white-dappled range of the Trinity Alps filled the horizon to the east and the mountains to the south hazed out in the sky. A lovely blue day. And yet something was missing, perhaps the chatter of the wilderness.

"There may be many things about this country that are appealing," Fletcher said, "but this is tough forage around here, and you don't see as much wildlife as you'd expect."

I have seldom experienced the quality of remoteness, of alienation from man-and-society, of not quite belonging, as here in the timbered hills.

We lunched under the Douglas firs beside the transparent turquoise of the tiny mountain pool, sharing our snack with a little trout near shore. A melting snowfield backdropped the lake's south shore and, incongruouslv, a lush field of wild onions lounged in the sun to the west.

"No Snowman here today, Monte," I said to Later.

"None today," he said, flicking a scrap of bread into the pool. "Today is for the trout. But if he had any sense this is where he'd be."

He glanced into the wildwood, and grinned. "It could be, though, that we're not the only ones observing strange fish out here."

This time I did not look over my shoulder.

There are certain points in life's small frenzies where the diplomatic thing to do is to settle for a stand-off.

This is what we may have achieved in the Siskiyou Mountains.

I didn't see the Abominable Snowman of California.

I am reasonably sure the Abominable Snowman didn't see me.

For nearly a week we explored the ranges, creeks, valleys, canyons and timber slopes of the Six Rivers National Forest country that is alleged to be the Bigfoot's sanctuary.

We saw tracks that—while intriguing—would likely be rejected in any laboratory trial on grounds they lacked clarity and were not offered as evidence at suitably ballyhooed press conferences.

Might there be an as yet-unclassified creature roaming those confined jungles, where the sun seems to shine only reluctantly?

Of course there might.

Is there?

I don't know.

Logic suggests that if there is something strange and new to science out there, it probably is another species of a known animal, a bear probably.

The irritation in this theory, however, is the fact that no bear known leaves footprints four feet apart.

"For the moment," said the party's wildlife sage, John Fletcher, "let us assume that the plaster casts we have seen are real—that is, authentic representations of prints actually made. And that those films are authentic, showing what purports to be a creature.

"If these things are truthful, then the creature is a human being. The foot suggests that, and the pictures show well-developed buttocks, breasts—all these things, together, consistent only with a conclusion that the thing is human.

"None of it, however, has been verified."

Continuing with the hypothesis, then, could a shaggy, seven-foot, human with flat feet and bad breath exist in northern California?

"As we have already observed," Fletcher said, "if it is going to be any place it will be California, which has a history of harboring unusual creatures.

"But to view the possibility on its merits: There is enough to eat in here, I suppose, to support a vegetarian, if that's what the creature is. In that connection, we probably explored the territory at a time of year slightly early. Later, there will be berries, to go with what I would assume to be the staple diet of a seven-foot vegetarian — maple shoots, willow bark, other edibles along the streams. Maybe, like man, he also does some non-licensed fishing.

"In other words, yes, he could support himself here. Maybe he migrates a little in the winter, but that concept is a little dizzy because he can't go much farther south than two counties, and even in California that isn't much of a migration."

"Still," I noted, "there are loggers around here who contend this is exactly what the Bigfoot does, winter in a mountained area not far from here called the Yollo Bolley."

"No doubt," Fletcher replied, "if there is anywhere in California where an Abominable Snowman winters it would have to be named Yollo Bolley."

And so what is the most forceful testimony pointing to the existence of something near-human in the Bluff creek waterways, or British Columbia, or the Himalaya, for that matter?

First, the pure weight of stories, legends, sightings, alleged sightings, tracks, track casts. In the Himalaya, certainly, something is there. Not a subhuman Yeti, perhaps, but an animal already classified, possibly the monkey-like languar, perhaps the recently-discovered blue bear—animals that make tracks that might have been distorted by the elements, melt, imagination or mythology into something inexplicable.

Secondly, there is support from some anthropology experts. There was an apelike race of giants, they argue, of which today's so-called Snowmen may be some dwindling remnant. There have been findings in Asia indicating creatures of ten to twelve feet tall once existed and that these might have sought sanctuary in the Southeast Asian mountains and, possibly, on the North American continent via the Alaskan land bridge in the glacial epoch.

Thirdly, not everybody who has claimed to have seen

tracks, or a creature, or a pelt, or photographed them, can be lying. Some tracks are phony, but not all people who find tracks are phony. There just are not that many liars per capita. A hard-headed explorer such as Peter Byrne clearly believes some of the tracks, and has subjected them to a very unromanticized scrutiny. If some of the Bigfoot tracks are real, then, we know of no animal on the North American continent that could have made them.

All right, let's say there is a near-human creature there. Are there many of them, a few of them?

One of them?

"There are too many tracks for it to be just one," a lumberjack said.

Well, how many of the tracks are authentically unexplainable?

Probably not many.

For years, you might remember, an Indian named Ishi lived in almost the very midst of a white settlement in California without being detected. When finally civilized, he was given some rudimentariy social lessons and quickly died.

Might the Snowman be some outcast or anti-social, possibly feeble-minded wanderer?

"There was a youngster who disappeared from his family years ago," one of the Hoopa Reservation merchants said, "an oversized boy who had seemed to be retarded. He was never heard from again. I don't believe in Bigfoot. But if you're going to believe it, maybe that's a theory as good as any."

Undoubtedly, it is as good as most, but still not quite acceptable. The generally-held impression among Bigfoot aficionadoes is that the creature is too big and too apelike to be a human being as we know human beings.

The anti-Snowman arguments are more tolerable. First,

there is too much of the man-from-Mars flavor in all of this—flying saucers, Paul Bunyan, the sandman and the bogeyman.

If so many people have seen him or seen his tracks, why isn't there some evidence of him around? Yes, yes, nature is supposed to dispatch the dead quickly in the wilderness, by way of scavengers, the elements, but if the thing is really there amid the many tracks it is alleged to have made, why haven't some remains been found?

Why hasn't one been captured or simply bowed to the psychedelic California environment and given himself up as a means of ending the unequal struggle?

There are stories that a captive wildman actually was viewed by a Red Army captain during World War II in the Caucasus, and the observations are there in military annals. No conclusion was drawn, however, and it was never ascertained whether the wildman was carrying a card.

We have heard a lot of fantasy, but no Abominable Snowman has ever been confronted by a human being in verifiable history.

We have seen pictures of a seven-foot creature that may have been a female Snowman, and yet the crested forehead of the creature is more consistent with male physiognomy than female.

Our expedition was not precisely scientific nor extensive, but it did observe the ground rules—as much, possibly, as any that has been in the Bluff Creek recently. In a week we covered something like 215 man miles along the creeks and in the forest.

Despite the fruitlessness of most of the creek-bed hunt, I cannot say it was a wasted interlude. The country is strange and possessive, but it aroused one. It invested him subtlely and surprisingly with a sense of discovery—a jeweled little waterfall around the canyon bend where he had expected only another log snag; a lone redbush in full bloom amid the sterility of the black canyon walls.

Yet this was the kind of outcast wilderness that never allowed one to forget he was an intruder. The creeks were still noisy and frothing although relatively tame when we forded them. A few weeks ago they were stampeding and ruthless, so strong that the flooding Bluff Creek itself plowed a canyon eighty feet deep, in three weeks, through the defenseless serpentine rock.

In there are animals big, wild and unmolested. What else is in there depends on your theory, your fantasy, your luck.

Man's legends do not vanish quickly nor does his wish to move one stride beyond what is demonstrable truth. This is why he looks at the stars, or into the jungle, or the Douglas fir wilderness of California.

Could there be some kind of Abominable Snowman of the mountains?

Your mind tells you no, but when you are sitting about the campfire and a vagrant breeze stirs the pines, and the fire ebbs—in this reference you may conclude:

Yes, Virginia, there could be.

Duet at the Met

Did the skittish hand of destiny thrust Alfredo Manuel Martini into the wrong Met, opera lovers?

I raise this question on the theory that only the arrival in town of the touring warblers from New York could have inspired Sunday's passionate aria of wrath from the baggy-trousered tenor who manages the Twins.

To get the same acoustic effect, the opera company is bringing its full entourage—temperamental coloraturas, glowering baritones, glockenspielers, terpsichoreans and a bullpen full of spearcarriers. At the very outside, however, all they can accomplish is to get two heroines stabbed, one garroted and another stiff from consumption.

Not one of the high-priced vocalists, however, will have the nerve to take on the whole Griffith organization, which Billy Martin managed yesterday afternoon. Not only that, but he did it *a cappella,* which the music culturists will tell you is without the benefit of a single chord from trainer Doc Lentz' second-hand guitar.

In other words, Martin winged it, without script, stage direction or an anguished soprano to whom he might have presented one of his flowering tomato plants as symbol of their frail togetherness. This against the assaults of the coarse conspirators represented by George Brophy and Sherry Robertson of the Twins' farm system.

"What Brophy's doing with the young pitchers," Martin declared in the midst of his raging half-hour recitative in his office, "is making an ass out of Billy Martin.

"If we win this thing—and we're going to—there's going

to be a helluva lot of changes around here next year. It doesn't bother me that I'm stomping on toes. What do they think they're doing to mine? You don't win, nobody cares about your excuses afterward. If they want the manager to manage scared, they got the wrong guy."

Close watchers of the road show Met will recognize instantly here the seeds of an operatic epic. There is the promise of the vendetta in there, a swatch of gauntlet-throwing defiance and even a little piece of gypsy fatalism. One imagines Billy leaning over a castle parapet in a timeless posture of torment, flinging resin bags on Brophy's bald head below as he sings the imperishable ballad "Go Jumpa in Minnetonka."

I know the opera world is rife with family feuds. The two resident tigresses, Renata Tebaldi and Maria Callas, were at it for years. There was the tenor here two years ago who threatened to throw a left hook at an uncouth basso profoundo. But these are lemonade wars alongside Martin's dressing room gunnery, which scattered grape-shot on practically all of the Twins' board heads except the chief boardhead himself, Calvin.

The non-baseball audience should be informed that Martin is involved in a game of bureaucratic pigeon-holes. In the Martin view there are too many Griffith-related bureaucrats and too many pigeon holes. Futher, the only indispensable bureaucrats are the manager, who is in charge of the players, and the owner, who is in charge of the manager.

Billy first indicated his displeasure with the system by throwing a right cross into the traveling secretary's jaw in 1966.

Still you have to richly admire the guy's unbreakable crust, don't you? The biographers of the other past and present managerial cyclones around here, the Dutchman and Wren Blair, talked affectionately about bluntness and gall; but here, people, is the one, the only, an original, and we better cherish Superbilly before he talks his way back to his ravioli kitchens.

So now we were in the Martin office. He sat there at his desk, the artist at bay, a brooding Toscanini in underwear. Brophy, he charged, had railroaded his young pitcher, Charley Waters, to Charlotte instead of a more prestigious incubator, Denver. "What the hell did Brophy ever play? To Charlotte, where Calvin's fraternity brother runs the team. No, don't blame Calvin. Everyone's trying to be the brother's keeper."

Martin stalked over to the cooker and speared a frankfurter midships, as though skewering Brophy on a point of order. The sausage gasped tragically, and Martin exited to face a fierce tomorrow.

Okay, Bill, but can't you wait until you get back into first place. I mean, the other guys have got some stock. All you've got is a lasagna tin.

Mr. Stenvig's Unbeatable Nominee

No matter how you voted, bet or rooted, you will have to credit Charlie Stenvig the policeman with launching a bold and surprising administration.

Within two hours after being certified as the new mayor of Minneapolis, Mr. Stenvig tossed a fresh thunderbolt at the groggy professional politicians by making his first appointment.

His chief adviser, Charlie announced, would be God.

Anybody else have a candidate before the nominations are closed?

Now nobody who knows the detective would question his absolute earnestness in this selection, or fail to be impressed by the humility with which it was announced.

But it does raise some provocative questions, such as what happens when the appointment comes up before the Council for confirmation?

Tell me how you would proceed, friends, if you were the Republican majority leader and had to ask the appointee for his qualifications.

No, I think we will have to agree the extraordinary officer has done it again, confounded the Courthouse insiders once more, routed the seasoned pols with the originality of this first decision.

Alongside Charlie's opening appointment, Nixon's widely advertised choice of Warren Burger seems downright dull. Burger, after all, is merely upright, conservative, honest, thrifty and Republican. He can't do a blessed thing about the rain.

And so Charlie has immediately disarmed his critics with the eminent reasonableness of his first appointment, a choice acceptable to almost all, I would guess.

This aside, the onlooker is powerless to know what Charlie's election portends for the city of Minneapolis. But he is fairly safe in assuming it will be analyzed by political sages from coast-to-coast with a wisdom and fervor that will make Mr. Stenvig the second most celebrated Charlie in the country overnight and maybe the first if they ground the Red Baron.

I leave it to the political oracles to determine whether Charlie's romping victory over Dan Cohen is a measure of the country's mounting resentment of social disorder, the agitation of youth for change, high taxes, unisex clothes, The Establishment or — for that matter — the early crabgrass season.

In some manner, Charlie DOES belong in the Peanuts strip somewhere, as the representation of national perplexity in this time of mingling affluence, revolution, three-car garages and Molotov cocktails.

Maybe Charlie belongs in there at a parking meter writing a ticket for reformers too hurried to drop in the nickels. I would imagine this is how his constituency might draw him today.

When all of the psychoanalysis is done with, though, it may well emerge that a vote for Charlie was simply a vote against the big shot — not Cohen, really, but the movers, the decision-makers, the newspapers, the political parties, the wheels.

In short, there are rare times when the anonymous breadmakers get the opportunity to cast a ballot not for the endorsee or the future senator or the party's annointed, but for themselves.

There is recent precedent, of course. The circumstances

may be different and certainly the geography, but the voters of Georgia did the same thing with Lester Maddox.

We may only hope the counterattack of democracy is more rewarding in Minneapolis than it has been in Georgia. Charlie, after all, does have the wary sense of humor of the professional cop.

This is assuring because most of the politicians in town and people who regard themselves as thinking moderates construe Stenvig's election not only as a first-magnitude political disaster but a civic embarrassment.

All of this may be overdrawn, as may be the forecasts for street violence ahead with the emergence of a man who has asked to have the handcuffs removed from the cops in their dealings with the disorderly.

The city HAS had law and order, by and large, and even more so under the Police Chief Donald Dwyer, an able and effective cop whose prospects in Stenvig's cabinet are not be as promising as those of Charlie's first appointee.

But by its own light — and who is to say it is all that misguided — the public gauges the point at which the middle-roaders seem to have been forgotten, imposed upon, sidetracked or just plain taxed to the eyeballs.

At this point it will vote for the amateur politician who is one of them. On second thought, Charlie's finesse in his early announcements suggest he may not be an amateur after all.

I mean when you beat the Republicans, Democrats, Richard Nixon, Gene McCarthy, The Minneapolis Star and Tribune, Dayton's and Dan Cohen in the same election, you just may be ready to turn pro.

Anyone for fingerprints?

Rebellion in the Composing Room

A mystified reader telephoned today, seeking an explanation for some strange, vagrant messages that have been appearing in her newspapers lately.

"I'm reading all about the storms and tornadoes," she says, "and when I'm halfway through here on Page 4 in the Thursday Star it's like I just opened a Chinese fortune cookie."

This made the bafflement unanimous because while I have heard Minnesota weather blamed on North Dakota, Canada and WCCO, I have never heard of it originating in a Chinese cookie factory.

"What I'm referring to," the caller explained, "is this section in the article that says:

" 'At Raymond, store windows were smashed, trees were uprooted, farm buildings collapsed and some livestock disappeared.'

"The next paragraph says:

" 'Help the starving Biafrans and Mpls. Newspaper printers.'

"What," she asks, "have the Minneapolis newspaper printers got to do with disappearing livestock and falling trees in Raymond?

"Further, I was reading the morning newspaper the other day all about the world's population and industrial growth, and it says:

" 'Less dramatic was the world's agricultural production with a gain of 26 percent and, due to the population increase, a per capita gain of only 4.1 percent.'

"Then it says, 'Star and Tribune printers have been con-
sistently underpaid,' after which the story goes on to say
'In Africa, the per capita food output rose only 1 percent
. . .'

"Kindly," the lady adds, "illuminate me as to the origin
of all this surprising information. Who is sending these
anguished messages from the cookie factory — the printers,
the editors or the publishers?"

Well, now. Without trying to judge the merits of the
argument, I think it is safely discernible that we have
here what the mediators call a certain lack of rapport between the management and printers of the Minneapolis
Star. In short, the boys are negotiating.

I would guess the fugitive paragraphs to which the lady
refers represent an imaginative new approach by the
printers to the art of indirect contract negotiation, a sort
of deflective bargaining.

The very least you can say about it is that the publication is now becoming a truly people's newspaper, meaning practically anybody can get into it.

I would be less than candid if I did not point out that
the situation has caused a small amount of hair-pulling
by some of the authors around here, most of them union
members themselves. The hazard, of course, is whose soaring literature is going to be shot down next by the sportive
vigilantes downstairs.

Now personally, I have to say my relations with both
sides in these negotiations have been good. The company's
management has been reasonable in meeting my grocery
bills and the printers have rescued me from time to time
when I have misspelled words and thus helped preserve
my record of having gone eight straight years without
making an error.

And so I have no particular personal fear of intruding

on this intramural squabble and trust that my friends among the printers will continue to handle my material with devoted ETOAin SHRDULE, bx z, bx, bx, ETOAIN SHRDLU

You have to understand it take lɔng years of cultivating these relationships, involving a sense of understan . . . The QUICK BROWN FOX JUMPED OVER THE LAZY DOG'S BACK; THE QUICK BROWN DOG JUMPED AROUND THE LAZY FOX;

 I will grant that it is sometimes hard to draw the line, in a struggle of maneuver such as this, between heavy-handed mischief and light-fingered malice. Lifetime students of corporate combat come to recognize the difference between snipery and gunnery. It's like the suitor who sprinkled essence of garlic into his rival's atomizer. It may not be lethal but it's awfully tough to explain when you're trying to score points.

Now a few might ask, "Well, even if some of the boys have furtively slipped type into the news stories, can't this be detected?" The answer is 'yes and no,' but the only fool-proof system would be for the liaison editor to stand on his head in the composing room for eight hours in order to read the type, and this is longer than the record for this activity, held jointly by two assistant city editors.

But it gets back to the mutual regard that has been built up over the years between the journalists and printers. Almost all of us are vulnerable, but not many of us really have to worry about printers horning in with dippy messages.

Columnists are defined as typographical mistakes waiting to be corrected.

Through most of this sparring, one has to commend the paper's management on its restraint and refusal to en

Help feed and counsel the harrassed publishers, of The

Minneapolis Star.

Like I said, it has to be based on mutual rega ETOKin Shrdule . . .

Mr. Blair Blows a Gasket

By the shakiest of margins, the republic has been saved for at least another two days from the catastrophe of a new resignation by the coach of the North Stars hockey team, Wren Blair.

This temporary reprieve took the form of a 3-2 North Stars' victory over St. Louis Sunday and coincided — as a matter of fact it provoked — a milepost moment on Sunday afternoon television, when all of the announcers were struck speechless simultaneously.

Only Blair could stop television, at least the audio portion of it. For those only loosely familiar with this extraordinary man, we will provide a quick scenario to let you know how narrowly we escaped a national trauma.

Blair was born under the sign of Aggravatius the Agitator. In the politics of hockey he is a type of blueline bolshevik, specializing in incitement to riot, apoplectic hand-wringing, moody martyrdom and impromptu hysterics. Nobody has ever done a better job of agonizing in public since John Brown, who matched Blair as a revolutionary but never drew as many bench penalties.

A year ago Blair began by trying to blow up not the officials but the customers. "There's nothing wrong with Minnesota crowds," he admitted, "that a little honest-to-God unsportsmanlike conduct wouldn't cure. You're nothing but a bunch of phlegmatic Swedes."

This roiled our sensitive national prides, since it made no allowance for all of the phlegmatic Norwegians, Germans and Icelanders, who certainly deserved equal billing with the Swedes.

Having indicted the ticket buyers as sheep, Blair pivoted briskly in the pasture a few months later and denounced his athletes as lambs. Whereupon he quit as coach in November to devote his full scholarship to general managing, trying stubbornly although not very successfully to conceal his all-around brilliance from a knowing public.

Bowing to popular clamor, Blair returned as coach in January with a ceremonial laying on of hands. This appeased the public and absolutely terrified the Stars, who have to deal with Blair not in heaven but at contract time.

The conversion was immediate. The athletes began to win or at least to tie, which in the NHL, I understand, is even more practical. The club now finds itself in an excruciating squeeze to make the playoffs, which everybody in hockey is supposed to make or throw himself into the Great Slave Lake in disgrace.

Blair has responded to this summit challenge with a scriptural rage against the officials that puts Wren right in there with Huey Long, Mrs. Butler and Joseph Goebbels. Blair imagines his team encircled by fate and zebra-striped dragons.

"It seems," he revealed after tieing St. Louis a week ago, "that they have a conspiracy against us. Their whole attitude is one of arrogance."

Four days later the Stars tied again, at Montreal. "The referee," he declared, "took that win right away from us." This left the Stars trailing the officials by two points when they returned in fury to Minneapolis. Here they once more tied, and Blair all but expired. He writhed. He screamed. He demanded the officials' heads and condemned their souls. His color coursed through the spectrum with each stroke of injustice, moving from natural scarlet to owly magenta and on to convulsive purple.

"They hooked and they held and they grabbed in the last seven minutes but the officials weren't going to call it," he pleaded. "We just can't get a break. I may step out as coach if it keeps going this way."

Somewhere in the Great Rink up there high near Hudson's Bay, somebody must have heard. And he produced an epochal hour in the history of television, when all available announcers ran out of superlatives.

Cesare Maniago, the North Star goalie, turned back shot on shot in St. Louis. The announcer already had revealed there were at least two immortals, goalies Glen Hall and Jacques Plante, on the St. Louis roster. The color announcer now discovered a third immortal, defenseman Doug Harvey.

It looked bad because the Stars were out-immortaled 3-0. But Maniago's performance began to stir the broadcasters. They started calmly enough by describing him as indescribable. From there they went to unbelievable.

It was now a contest. What WAS Maniago. He kicked out more shots. "Maniago," one of them disclosed, "is superb, he is impregnable, he is relentless." This made you wonder whether he was coming or going. Finally, after one especially acrobatic effort, the announcer of record announced, exhausted:

"I am out of words. I really cannot go beyond unbelievable."

Come on, friend, how about . . . well . . . immortal?

Demise of the Hammock

For weeks I have been both intrigued and appalled by the sales campaign of Gabberts furniture store, aimed at plopping the married couples of America onto king-sized mattresses.

No doubt you are familiar with this Cloud Nine, far-horizons style of bedding, so large that sleepwalkers are now able to jog nine or ten laps without getting out of bed and may even — if they are transported into a TV football dream sequence — try kicking the extra point.

My argument here is that while the supersize mattress has improved our mobility, it may cost us dearly in congeniality. In other words, aren't we faced with a new threat to the institution of marriage, to the casual and accidental undercover collisions that have sparked and illuminated this age of adventure?

Isn't it better to risk a spontaneous elbow in the rib cage than to have to keep separate alarm clocks to allow for the difference in time zones?

And isn't it true that man-wife relations through the ages have been tied closely to the size and style of bedroom furniture? In the caveman days of civilization, for example, when they slept in bearskins, there may have been a lingering muskiness around the household, but divorce courts were virtually unheard of.

On the other hand, the onset of Nero, Mark Anthony, 20th Century Fox and other decadents popularized the emperor-sized bed for the first time 2,000 years ago, and the result was the recline and fall of the Roman Empire to the forces of Attila, who used thatched sleeping bags.

Profiting from this lesson of history, many of the early American settlers slept in crude hammocks. This made the evening unpredictable for the marrieds of those days, to be sure, and while cozy, it did present additional technical problems. But whoever heard of a squirrel-shooter paying alimony or going bankrupt in consultant's fees?

"I can live with the sacroiliac," the old frontiersman used to say, "as long as she don't garnishee my pelts."

It was against this backdrop of history that I walked into Gabbert's mahogany fantasyland on 69th and France yesterday afternoon in response to a radio commercial declaring Gabbert's as the home of "qualified and well trained men in the bedding department."

I was greeted by the owner and president, Don Gabbert, and one Bob Kearney, who is the chief sandman in the company's bedding department. They were smiling and had their hands clasped lightly before them, a posture which always puts me on guard. It is the stance into which my pals in the undertaking business fall instinctively at Kiwanis meetings, leaving you to wonder whether they are socializing or speculating.

"Mr. Gabbert," I said, "I'm sure these are extremely comfortable mattresses and very functional, but don't you see here some peril for married couples, wherein they may now need a switchboard and a part-time steno to communicate?"

"None whatsoever," he replied. "The reverse is true, if anything. Here you have a king-sized mattress, 76 inches in width and 80 inches in length. Do you have any idea how many millions of people have begun their day grouchy and bedraggled as a result of a crowded and generally disordered night on a mattress?"

I acknowledged not having examined this phenomenon. "But aren't you tending to polarize people this way?" I persisted, "to drive one into the wall and the other into the closet?"

"Not at all," he continued, "the popularity of the king-size mattress has worked to bring people back together, people who once were irritated by the congestion of the old standard size. As a result, more people than ever are sleeping together, by which I mean fewer couples today are using twin beds. What this new size does, of course, is to make sleeping more versatile. It gives you more options.

"Couples are now able to get themselves warm on a cold winter night and then withdraw independently to the comfort and roominess of what amounts to three feet of bed space for each. It's the bedroom version of what the gym teachers used to call free play. Diagonal sleepers can now indulge their acrobatics without evicting their mates. Here, I'll show you how utilitarian this is."

With this, Gabbert flung himself upon one of the king-sized mattresses and bounced happily into the air before settling again at a 45-degree angle.

"My dear fellow," I said, "your customers are shopping for a mattress, not a trampoline."

"We do not apologize," he explained, "for its natural springiness. We live in an age of athletics. The king-size is functional, therapeutic and ideal for diversionary games such as touch football and hopscotch. What it is is a full-service mattress."

Fold your hammocks, pals.

Radar Be Damned, Virtue Will Triumph

We have before the court today one of the most heart-clutching alibis ever presented to the Solomons of the municipal bench.

"I will tell the judge as I told the arresting officer," said Suzi Lane, in a ringing defense of her civil liberties, "that I was speeding to save my virtue."

Who can resist being drawn by the magnetism of this appeal and its speculative mystery? I find this defense not only poignant and urgent but, in this day and era, practically original. And yet you will admit a number of legal questions surface immediately.

Now there are some legal issues simply too crucial to be left to the judges. I will lay the facts before the public today, therefore, in the hope that we may reach some working concensus as to the credibility of Miss Lane's remarkable excuse, and its effect on the doctrine of presumptive innocence.

Miss Lane is a 23-year-old converted Braniff stewardess, currently blonde. Some time ago she developed a night club act in the San Francisco Casbah of North Beach. But, irritated by the amateur competition in the streets, she followed the prevailing winds to Minneapolis, where most of the night club competition consists of boilermaker-drinking contests and singing janitors.

Miss Lane is now employed by one of the more boisterous saloons in northeast Minneapolis, having changed runways from the International Airport's 10,000-foot asphalt strip to the saloon's 25-foot reformed shuffleboard. Miss

Lane does an antsy go-go dance clothed in high leather boots and luminescent trifles. She also sings on weekends when the crowd, in her judgment, "is ready for deeper art. Otherwise I stick with the acrobatics, and this may be the reason I got arrested."

Our investigation now turns to the nub of the case against Miss Lane. "I was leaving the place for my apartment in Bloomington," she recalls, "when I noticed three cars parked outside the bar. The guys in them seemed like motorcycle types. And how I got worried when I drove off at a pretty brisk speed and one car started following me.

"I was driving on Washington toward downtown and I kept accelerating well over the speed limit. I tell you I wasn't going to stop for any red light, either. But I finally did.

"You experienced a moment of repentance for your speeding?" I asked her.

"No," she replied, "the red light was behind me, and it was rotating on a police car."

In the timeless tradition of police officers, the traffic cop demanded the lady's driver's license and an explanation. In an eventful career on the force, the dedicated gendarme had heard speeding women plead hospital appointments, lovers' quarrels, cooking casseroles and stuck gas pedals, but never threatened virtue.

"He didn't believe you had sufficient foundation for a plea of innocence?" I asked dolefully.

"Now wait just a minute," Miss Lane objected. "All I said was he arrested me for going 35 miles an hour — actually it was more — in a 30-mile zone and then almost had a hysterical seizure when I said I was trying to outrun some of the customers who may have been that turned on by the show."

The officers observed no pursuing cars in sight, although admitting that in the confusion of our fashions and times the ardent customers may have gone after the drummer.

"The police cited me for speeding," she continued, "and left it to me to pay the $15 fine or fight the case in court. So I went down to City Hall, and I have a court appointment set for next week. Now there is no question that I was over the speed limit, and I intend to plead guilty, but I am going in there to ask the judge to look at my extenuating circumstances."

Wordlessly I considered Miss Lane and the implications of such a judicial review.

"All things considered," I advised at length, "I think you will be better off asking the judge to adhere strictly to the law and let his clerk consider your circumstances."

Having viewed her show, I would judge Miss Lane's strenuous gyrations might get her customers agitated but certainly not incriminated. My guess is that the lady has encountered livelier hazards in the pilot's cabin of a 727.

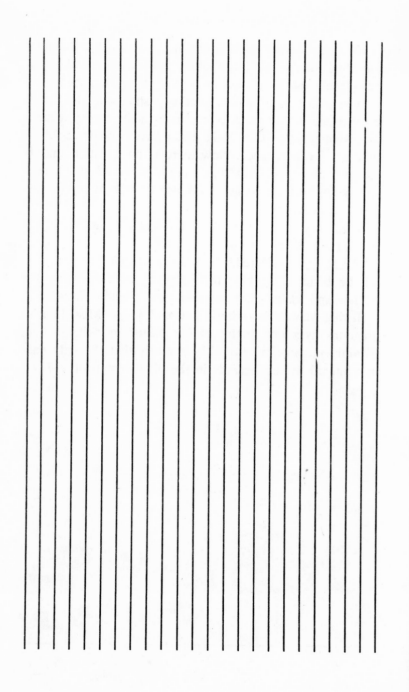

Last Reveille for a Soldier

The American people granted to Dwight Eisenhower an unwavering fondness and trust that made him a man beyond, an authentic and perhaps last-of-a-kind folk hero. His death March 28, 1969, occasioned not only a period of national mourning but a curious sort of public self-examination.

There was a quality in his expressive face that buoyed and comforted us and, in his last years, vaguely disturbed us because Dwight Eisenhower was not so much an image for the country as its conscience.

His was the America of our childhood visions, its elemental goodness, its forgiveness in the flush of victory and its earnest groping to do the right thing with its strengths and its gifts. And at the end, in a way his ardent but wandering rhetoric could never achieve, his death jars us into a truth — the realization of how far we have drifted from the disciplined and unapologetic codes that invested his voice with the simple moralities the world believed.

What matters most intimately to us is not the verdict of history but the verdict of the people who called him Ike.

In this it was not so important that millions loved him but that almost all trusted him. He was a warrior who never sought the role nor struck the pose of Olympian grandeur, a president who held the nation together not by any overwhelming wisdom or even leadership but by the unmistakable decency of his character.

No legend-makers were needed to spell these qualities

in capital letters. He had a directness from the Kansas prairie, a pride from the drill field, a faith from his family but mostly he had a sunny spontaneity that was all Ike and nobody else.

And while they gave him pluralities by the millions, the country's voters must have known that as president Ike was capable of muddling with the best of them.

Reporters regarded his press conferences as weekly exercises in bewilderment. The problem was not to discover where Ike ended a sentence but where he began. In his very resolute attempts to clarify his position, Ike would often start out trying to attack the question and wind up trying to surround it.

This produced a kind of oratory by end run which the journalist delighted in spoofing—but never too hard nor too wisely, because the man's hold on the nation's affections was that strong and his sincerity that compelling.

He was best when he could stand before us and talk with the old West Point fervor about God and country and honor. In the hands of another man the words might ring dull and contrived. But in Ike's they were the flesh of life, and we understood it.

Which probably explains why he was weakest when immersed in the intrigues of Cold War diplomacy and why he seemed so embarrassed and ineffectual when called to book by the shoe-pounding Nikita Khrushchev after the U-2 incident.

But it was as a soldier that history will judge him most generously, a life that commanded his deepest passion, and — in the final years of his life — caused him the deepest dismay in the rising defiance of authority around him.

There was something altogether knightly about the man that we are not likely to see again on the American scene.

The social convulsions, which he merely began to deal with, will not permit it. The times may require a different and more imaginative kind of leadership, a willingness to bend the rules, to accommodate, but for all of that there is still no political substitute for what is in a man's heart. Ike fought death stubbornly and without lavish public heroism. He soldiered just that way. He was the man in command at our most profound military hour, who led millions through the Armageddon of Normandy and stirred in us a lifting pride and national unity of a kind we have not again experienced.

Beyond all of this, however, he was a good and true man, and he takes from us a personal kind of honor and love we have conferred on no other man.

We should not blush to say it. He was an American soldier.

Washington, D.C. — The great granite stillness of the cathedral swallowed his small words of tenderness as he stood before the flag-hung casket of his fallen general.

He was an unknown soldier, a 47-year-old power lineman from Cleveland, the son of a coal miner. The lines of mourners moved about him, and he seemed hesitant to pause for a private devotional, however brief.

His name was Mike Eloff, a rifleman in the 90th Division in Normandy. He had seen Dwight Eisenhower only once, at a training beach inspection in England one month before the Normandy invasion.

Twenty-five years ago Mike Eloff waded through the cauldron of D-Day's second assault wave — its gales and body-strewn breakers and machine-gun fire — in the forefront of history's mightiest invasion force.

He had survived it, survived shrapnel wounds and later the Bulge in Belgium. Their memory, once frightening, had hazed with the years, but now he stood behind the red velvet cordon in Washington's National Cathedral and he groped for some gesture of pride, some simple eloquence to tell his two teen-age sons beside him how it had been to serve under the general.

This he could not find. He could only tighten his hands on their shoulders and move on.

His red-weathered face is not normally solemn and later he smiled in the awareness of his obscurity.

"Just a dog-face," he said, "like millions of others, a draftee. I wasn't any military man like the good one who is lying there in the church. I didn't know him, so I can't really be churned up inside like the people who did know him.

"Still, he was such an honest-to-God type of guy, wasn't he? He was the kind of guy you wanted to walk up to and shake hands with.

"You know, I think that is what I was doing today."

This was the unshakeable bond, the enduring fondness between Ike and his public that brought out tens of thousands on this cheerless grey day of the riderless horse and the casket-bearing caisson.

For all of Eisenhower's popular adulation when he lived here and his two terms in the presidency, this was not his province. He was a son of the Corps and his passion was West Point. The men in blue business suits he may have called colleagues but it was the men in olive drab he called comrade.

And it was from these that Ike Eisenhower received the most emotional salute Sunday as his body, borne gently by an honor guard of enlisted men, was lifted from its rest-ing place in Bethlehem Chapel to the hearse.

Here were the Joint Chiefs of Staff, the grimly-erect honor guard, aging warriors with whom Ike fought, J. Lawton Collins — and General of the Army Omar Bradley.

They had been classmates at West Point, had counseled each other, had each in his personal fashion advanced to generalship — Bradley with his quiet tactical brilliance, Eisenhower with his ability to manage and influence people, his administrative flair and his likeability.

Bradley had been his right arm in Tunisia, in the sweep through France, his confidante in the pre-presidential years. He understood Dwight Eisenhower's flaws but never underestimated his friend's prairie toughness, the force of honesty and morality or the allure of his instictive warmth.

These, he would say, were what made Ike a great and good friend.

Now it was 3:05 Sunday and Mrs. Eisenhower had arrived at the church on the arm of her son, and the honor guard was carrying Dwight Eisenhower's casket toward the hearse.

Slowly, the Coast Guard Band played "Onward Christian Soldiers" as the processional moved past Omar Bradley. The wind snapped at the American flag above the coffin and for one imperishable moment, as the old soldier stood at attention with his hand trembling in salute, the two were together in one final reunion, the unbreakable comradeship of the battlefield.

Above them the cathedral's death knell gonged with doleful finality. There would be no more reunions for the generals.

For the Mike Eloffs, the memory is less intimate, the grief less anguishing.

"All I know," the private from the coal fields said, "is

that on June 6th in 1944 he had my life in his hands. He could have said, 'It's off, the weather's bad,' and who knows what might have happened. But I'll tell you one thing I remember about that day.

"I wanted him to say, 'Let's go.' And he did. The way the weather was, I thought he must have been out of his mind.

"They musta taught a steady hand of poker in Abilene."

W ASHINGTON, D.C. — The clatter of busy sightseers in the huge, vaulted rotunda of the Capitol has yielded on this melancholy afternoon to the silent massed galleries of the great of government.

Sen. Edward Kennedy is one of the first to arrive, towering in the front row of the Senate section beside the nattily groomed Hugh Scott of Pennsylvania, the frail and monastic Mike Mansfield of Montana and Everett Dirksen, the tousled comic-tragedian of the Senate.

In the hour and half of waiting ahead others will exchange small talk and a few will smile, but Kennedy will never let himself forget that he has stood here before in a deeper, more personal grief, and he will not break his silence.

Banks of tripodded cameras run the muraled curvature of the rotunda walls beneath the soaring dome of the nation's statehouse where eight presidents have lain on the black-mantled catafalque in the center of the amphitheater.

The body of Dwight Eisenhower, borne by Army caisson, will arrive within the hour.

The cordoned media sections fill quickly. Some of the newspaper corps, recalling the rites of a nation numbed with horror by the martyr's death of a young president six years ago, seek to compare the moods.

"Television," one says, "has struck a tone of deep, sorrowing reverence which I can understand but which just does not seem to be there in the nation today — not disrespectfully, but because Ike was old and weakening, and the end was expected."

But the reverence is there, all right, not in a sudden sweep of national conscience but in the steady warmth of affection in which the country had held him and which did not have to be measured.

The limousines preceding the caisson and the riderless horse begin emptying the mourners of rank and celebrity.

The shah of Iran, clanking medals and saber in his ceremonial uniform, walks solemnly across the rotunda to a place in the section for visiting heads of state. "He's my kind of shah," a journalist remarks airily, echoing a familiar Capitol bon mot.

The processional is late, and the respectful silence in the great room has given way to a conversational undertone in which the still strikingly handsome Louis Montbatten of Britain now joins, relieving the strain of the foreign diplomatic corps around him.

Chief Justice Earl Warren, grim and fatigued, enters the hall at the head of his court, minus only Justice Douglas. Governors follow, and now stillness once more engulfs the rotunda as the uniformed Joint Chiefs of Staff enter and the chords of "Hail to the Chief" become audible from the Capitol steps.

Mrs. Mamie Eisenhower, her face unable to mask the struggle of the last three days, enters on the arm of her son, John, walks with him to the head of the Eisenhower family and chooses to stand for the ceremony.

Tenderly, the honor guard places the casket on the catafalque, and Richard Nixon takes a few steps forward to speak the nation's requiem for Ike.

He seeks to achieve a conversational tenor, to invest this last farewell with fondness and esteem and gratitude, at the same time trying to avoid a ponderous gloom.

The opening moments of his eulogy seem to fortify Mamie Eisenhower but now she closes her eyes momentarily and her fragile face reflects her struggle for control.

Mr. Nixon tries to help her with the informality of his style but her eyes moisten and her lips tremble when the President tells of the couple's last words together, how Ike had professed once more how much he loved his wife, his children, his grandchildren and his country.

John Eisenhower moves nearer to her, almost imperceptibly.

He was a man from Abilene, Mr. Nixon is saying, who touched something fundamental in America. He was a product of its soils and ideals, loved and followed not so much for what he did but for what he was.

Quite unconsciously, the President says, Dwight Eisenhower might have defined the uniqueness of his strength and the depth of his personal power and leadership when he began a talk to wartime Britain with the words, "I come from the heart of America . . ."

He was there again Sunday, and today, and it is unimaginable that he ever will really leave.

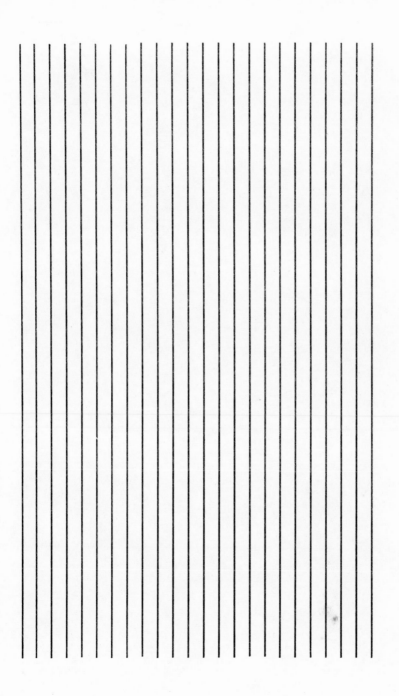

Old Faithful by Snowmobile

For three months of the year the 3,400 square miles of America's oldest and most spectacular national park swarms with tourists, panhandling bears and souvenir hawkers. In the winter Yellowstone is frozen in silence and solitude, a white wilderness rarely intruded by man. Until a few years ago it was largely inaccessible in midwinter. The advent of the snowmobile, however, has opened it to the winter adventurer.

It came gushing out of the snowfields and lava mounds, frothing and churning and noisy but fastidiously on time. As a showman Old Faithful may be an old act, but it is no prima donna.

In summer it is the centerpiece of the world's biggest natural freak show, the sulphur-and-steam carnivals of Yellowstone National Park.

In July it fumes and frolics for thousands at a time. In winter it plays to empty acres—except that today in early February it was attended by a quilt-clothed audience of snowmobilers who seemed an intrusion on the eerie anarchy of nature around them, the hot vapors and geysers of Yellowstone rising above the snow and ice-hung pines.

It might have been the sunrise of creation. It had a kind of alien beauty that stirred and baffled the viewer and gave him a sense of triumph at the same time because he did not have to face the customary stampede by regiments of camera fanatics.

I can take Yellowstone or leave it in the summer, and

usually leave it hastily when the traffic jams set me pining for the relative tranquility of Hennepin and 7th at 5 p.m.

Yellowstone in the winter, however, must be one of the most dramatic sights on earth.

Its immense snowfalls, height and geography kept it shut off to all but a few snowshoers and park rangers until the snowmobile mechanics discovered a new field for adventure here. And quite suddenly, a ride through the thermal spectacles and the great pine forests of Yellowstone has become one of the new passions of the western outdoorsman.

Among the aficionadoes of the cult are a group of businessmen and snow machine jockeys from the Idaho village of St. Anthony, where a climbing confederate of mine, Monte Later, operates a grocery store.

"I understand," Later telephoned some time ago, "there are people out where you live who get excited snowmobiling around Lake Minnetonka."

I confessed there were a few, most of whom usually stayed sober.

"The snowmobiler hasn't lived," Later said, "until he has driven the mountains of Idaho and run along the Firehole River in Yellowstone Park."

"The question is," I replied, "whether he'll still be alive when it's over."

"All you need," he said, "is thermal underwear, arctic boots, a snowmobile suit and plenty of gas."

As a running mate I retained the Minneapolis restaurant and saloon magnate, Joe Duffy, who distinguished himself on the return from Old Faithful by running out of gas and becoming the only snowmobiler in the short history of Yellowstone's winter commerce to fall asleep at the throttle while moving at thirty miles an hour.

There are two principal jump-off points for a snow tour

of Yellowstone, the resort town of West Yellowstone and the motor inn at Mammoth in the northern section of the park, the only lodge open year around in the park.

Later rounded up some of his business cronies, quartered them overnight in cabins near West Yellowstone and drove us from Idaho Falls to a truck stop near the resort.

We unloaded our borrowed snowmobiles from a pickup truck at 1:30 in the morning, got one started but failed to generate any enthusiasm in the other. A 50-mile-an-hour wind was blowing over the flats off the shoreline of frozen Henry's Lake.

"Where are we going if we get the snowmobile started?" I asked Later.

"A mile up the mountain side to a cabin where they are waiting for us with elk and antelope meat," he said. "We've got a near blizzard here, but I think we can make it if we don't lose the way. On the other hand, we can say to hell with the whole thing tonight and get some sleep."

"What's the nearest town," I asked.

"Last Chance, Idaho."

"Last Chance for what?"

"It depends," he said, "on your most urgent needs."

We slept.

But the weather cleared at daybreak and Later's 11-man expedition left West Yellowstone at 10 a.m., signed the ranger's register at the park gateway and schussed into Yellowstone toward Old Faithful 28 miles away.

Except for a small section near Mammoth, Yellowstone's highways are closed in winter. Snowmobile trails to Old Faithful and the Grand Canyon of the Yellowstone are maintained by the Yellowstone Park Co., the private concessionairre which operates winter tours in enclosed 12-passenger Bombardier snowmobile coaches.

We followed the route of the main highway from West

Yellowstone to Madison Junction. The trail was good, safe and comfortable. For miles we rode escort for the Firehole River, running through forests of Engleman spruce and lodge pole pine and then through the flats where hot springs and geysers flung up fragile clouds of steam.

Herds of elk loafed along the Firehole. The sky was beige, flattening the snow-light along the river. Two Trumpeter swans glistened below us, elegantly coursing the river among the snowy boulders.

We stopped often shutting off our engines to hear the sounds of the forest. I would not have imagined the intimate fulfillment of this country in the winter. In the summer it is a galloping sweepstakes of people, bears and automobiles. Today it was an idyll of snow and wildlife and— when we mercifully turned off the engines—silence.

It is attainable at some expense to the non-natives, but nothing exorbitant. We rode individually, for example, on snowmobiles that can be rented for $20 to $25 for a day's driving, guide included if necessary.

For those who prefer their touring by bus, fare on the 12-passenger cruiser is $15 from West Yellowstone to Old Faithful and $20 to the Grand Canyon of the Yellowstone.

A three-day package tour, Twin Cities to Yellowstone via Northern Pacific railway costs between $100 and $123 for an adult, the price including round trip rail fare, all meals in the itinerary, three nights lodging at Mammoth Motor Inn, and one bash-type party.

We, however, dispensed with the party on the day we rode to Old Faithful, postponing that in favor of a picnic of wieners, cheese and coffee at the lip of Old Faithful.

I timed the geyser between eruptions—62 minutes, right on the money.

Impishly, and because I felt the park owed me something for all of the summertime road jams, I walked up to the edge of the geyser's crater and looked down. It had been fifteen minutes since its last eruption and I had no anxieties.

Unaccountably, it started rumbling underneath.

I took off through the powdered snow in great and dedicated haste.

"Brother," Duffy said, "consider yourself lucky. That's a helluva way to take a sauna."

If You're a Boozer, Admit It

The Brassrail Alumni at Alcoholics Anonymous confront us today with a realistic new test for chronic boozers, both actual and aspiring.

I commend it to your attention as a means of removing the easy alibis and casual hypocrisy from your cocktail blenders and ask whether you might not save yourself some money and maybe a home by putting an as-yet unpublished telephone number into the hands of some promising soak of your acquaintance.

For this I am acting as a kind of unpledged conscript for the local AA cell, which discovered a while back that I disavowed the heady grape a couple of months ago and am now living a life of absolute clearheaded tedium.

Lacking the missionary's passion in these things, I do not necessarily recommend this rash and admittedly antisocial step to everybody. Most drinkers should have the maturity to judge whether their particular pace makes liquor a refreshment, a lift, an annoyance or a compulsion.

To the extent that it might be instructive to those who are not quite sure about classifying themselves, I might note my own deliberations of a few months ago. The conclusion: My normal cruising speed was several jiggers removed from what the reformers would describe as obsessive, but at the very least, you would give me high grades for consistency.

I think it is academic to argue whether drinking is a disease, a psychosis, an escape or a tax dodge. The argument has the virtue of keeping a number of magazine sup-

plement writers employed and does present a convenient
forum for professional confessionists. This calling used to
be limited to rehabilitated Communists, drunks and drug
addicts but has now been expanded to include glamorous
new entries such as married priests and diary-writing defensive linemen.

As a result, the Alcoholics Anonymous people find themselves increasingly upstaged in the competition to find
audiences that can be truly shocked. This is regrettable,
because their particular cult of evangelism may be the most
worthy and valuable of all in today's society.

Whether their stubborn propagandizing had anything to
do with it, I now find myself in a predicament where I
have (a) given up liquor (b) given up smoking and (c)
given up most caloric foods. All of this considerably nar-
rows the range in which a man may do some legitimate
hell-raising and dissipating, yet it does tend to calm the
corporate anxieties of the Coca-Cola people, who manu-
facture Fresca and Tab.

You may regard this as a confining life, but it should be
pointed out you can always switch to Sanka coffee, and
over the past few weeks therefore I have developed a quiet
pride in the effortless ambidextry with which I approach the
bar. I mean I can go either way, Fresca or Tab, and it
doesn't matter a shred whether the bartender is right or
left-handed.

The essential thing here is that you don't have to change
your social fraternities, abandon your friends, or indulge in
the silly affectations of Catawba juice parties. There is a
calm peace of mind and a loftily smug superiority in being
able to stride up to the bar and declare "a double Tab, on
the rocks." You will be regarded as some sort of physio-
logical fluke, but you can always tell the bartender,
"Friend, this stuff is a lot safer than booze, although I

admit it doesn't have quite the character."

I think it takes no special display of will power to stay off the stuff, beyond the normal impulses for survival, but it does take a little ingenuity at the stadium tailgate balls. Still, there are those who could use a hand. For these, AAA now has formed its locals into a Minneapolis-suburbanwide organization called Intergroup, whose serv- ices are instantly on call.

The standard test for alcoholism, you may remember, has been the Johns Hopkins exam which, in some ways, is impractical. Most drinkers, alcoholic or not, flunked it— ad agency drinkers, sororities and embalming associations. The copy desk of The Star, for example, flunked it unani- mously, coasting at the finish and using its third team for the final ten questions.

But now ask yourself this new set of questions: Do you think about drinking when doing something else? Do you, after a couple of drinks, start to gulp them faster? Do you drink by yourself at times? Do you have trouble remem- bering the next morning? Are you unsteady and trembling the next morning? Do your parents and mate complain about your drinking? Does it give you trouble with your job? Are your children aware? Do you have to juggle finances? Can you "stay on your feet with the best?" Do you postpone unpleasant duties and have a drink? Do other people comment on the screwball things you did and said? Do others have a hard time keeping up with you? Are others at work conscious of your drinking?

If you answer yes four times or more, you might do yourself a favor and dial 333-4247 in Minneapolis, 222- 1182 in St. Paul.

The Birds Collide with the Bees

The most alarming development in the brawl over sex education is the intervention of the inspired law-givers from that earnest fog mill in St. Paul, the Minnesota Legislature.

There are certain things the Legislature does well unaided. It used to do a very thorough job covering the clock and still enjoys a relatively high rank in the legislative science of happy dawdling.

We all have a right to be jittery whenever the Legislature gets into the general subject of sex, however, because by following their natural impulses there is always a clear and present danger that the solons might:

1. *Make it illegal.*
2. *Postpone it indefinitely.*
3. *Slap a tax on it.*

Any of these contingencies could work hardships on the body politic. The Legislature, to be fair, had to be pushed into the sex education controversy against its wishes. There is a shortage of certified lobbyists on this question in the Capitol, and in these circumstances the Legislature normally is at a loss to know how to vote.

As a result, the legislators' first reaction when they started hearing about sex a couple of weeks ago was to break into tears. Whether this unusual procedure was caused by anonymously planted tear gas or the very moving testimony of the witnesses, we shall never know.

Despite these weepy auspices, the Legislature is moving toward passage of a bill that would seek standards for the sex teachers — which is pretty fundamental and overdue; and permit parents to withdraw their kids from such classes — a clause that heightens the strife by infuriating the professional educators.

The problem is to assert some sense of moderation amid all the galloping piety and flights of martyrdom around us. But it's tough.

Having been present in fume-filled rooms after political campaigns of deep intrigue and savagery, and in football dressing rooms after last-second defeats, I had considered myself attuned to most of the ferocious language and postures of the times. Alongside the sex education rally, people, a Van Brocklin dressing room is Victorian.

For students of the rhetoric of damnation, however, it is a treasure house of original invective. Where else could you find this sapphire of vituperation, that "anyone who would deliberately arouse the child's curiosity or stimulate his unready mind to troubled sexual pre-occupations ought to have a millstone tied around his neck, and cast into the sea."

Now this does not leave the struggling educators a great deal of room for maneuver and not even much seaweed to hang onto. There is even less when the enraged orators come with the statistics. To quote once more:

"Sweden (is) a horrible example of unrestricted sex education and pornography in the schools, (where) the results have been totally and completely catastrophic, (converting) the Swedish children into moral vegetables (and creating) in these kids an obsession with sex that is consuming their lives."

This puzzles me on two counts. The first dates back to a visit to Stockholm a couple of years ago when I would have sworn I saw teen-age kids at least pausing in their lechery to go fishing in the Saltsjoen, while others were practicing hockey in a nearby lot to learn how to hold down the score in their annual romp over the more upright American kids.

The second involves a report I have before me from Keokuk High School in Iowa, where sex education has been taught on a voluntary basis since the early 1940s. Among girls who took the course, it tells us, the illegitimate birth rate is 15 times lower than among those who didn't; and among boys who took the course, the divorce rate has been nearly seven times lower than for those who did not.

Now I share the normal distrust of statistics, and I grant the scholars who declined the Iowa course may have been taking their alternative study hall in a hayloft. But I do recommend the Iowa survey to all angry crusaders, at least between indictments.

There is no question, though, that we have discovered a new participant spectacle to match Friday night bowling. In Edina, sex dialogues outdraw the Hornets. In Hopkins they pull in more than the raspberry festival. The sense of outrage, on both sides, is clearly sincere and dramatic, reaching a sweeping climax with declaration by a speaker in Robbinsdale that the schools now plan to spend 13 years teaching what can be taught about sex in 13 minutes.

It does leave one to wonder about the career of Johann Sebastian Bach, who had 22 kids and whose life therefore was one mad whirl between basinets and minuets. "Imagine," he was heard to say in later years, "how much more proficient I would have been if we had sex education classes in Salzburg."

Memorial Day, 1968

In thousands of city squares and village cemeteries today, the nation made its annual testament of debt to the men who have fallen under its flag.

The graveside litanies included the name Vietnam, its victims enrolled among the honored dead.

For all of the solemnity and Memorial Day oratory, however, unspoken questions hovered over this hour of requiem.

How much honor is there in death in Vietnam in 1968, in a grubbing, dirty war that has divided the nation, set off campus riots, driven the country's President to renounce another term, killed 23,000 American men and wounded more than 200,000 others?

Is there the same sense of national gratitude and pride in the battlefield sacrifice of the fighting man who wears the country's uniform today as there was twenty-five years ago in Guadalcanal and eighteen years ago in Seoul, and what do these doubts mean to the fighting man in Vietnam?

None of these questions could be evaded today, at a time when millions in the country do not believe there is need for American death in Vietnam.

Is today an empty memorial for the dead in Vietnam?

"I served as an officer in World War II," said a Minneapolis judge. "But then the country was absolutely unified. The war began with an act, Pearl Harbor, that enraged the entire country. There was never any question of national purpose, of the life-and-death nature of the war to the American people.

"There might be a hundred things that might bother or

scare you, but at least you never had the burden of knowing that some people at home were sneering at what you
were doing; or that there really was some doubt about the
morality of what you were doing.

"I tell you, I would hate to be fighting in Vietnam with
some of those things in the back of my mind. That and
knowing that for political and strategic reasons we really
aren't able to strike at the enemy with all of the power we
have. It must be a maddening state of mind for the in-
fantryman over there."

Is it?

For some, undoubtedly. But the evidence indicates that
American forces have fought in Vietnam with a vigor and
distinction to match their battleground performance of
World War II.

What is the incentive?

This is a Minneapolis Marine sergeant talking now, a
veteran of two years combat in Vietnam. He has killed
many. Some of those he has killed unwittingly, he admits,
were friendly South Vietnamese.

"When the shooting starts," he says, "all that counts is
discipline and training and pride and your instinct for
survival. You don't worry about people tearing up their
draft cards or politicians running for this on Vietnam or
that. If you have been trained right, you do what you're
told, and if the outfit is good, you'll probably come out
of it.

"I don't have any pipe dreams about what it's all about
in Vietnam. The South Vietnamese troops just won't fight.
I don't care how you want to spell it, that's what it is. The
North Vietnamese have the morale and the will to fight.
The whole country would be better off if we let Ho Chi
Minh run it. The South Vietnamese don't have any leaders,
and they've got to keep us there.

"Don't ask me how we're going to get out of it. The guys might as well get ready for bigger fights ahead. We go into this valley and out of that one, but those trails still run through Laos and Cambodia, and we can't touch them there.

"Yes, we try to be good-will people to the civilians and the kids in Vietnam, and try to patch some people here and there, but it's still a war with guns and if a man is made of the right stuff he'll get himself ready for the fire-fight. And when he's walking through the rice paddies with his rifle, he ain't thinking about all that trouble in the streets back home or how many people think the war is right in the latest Gallup Poll.

"All he's thinking about is doing what he's told and coming out of it alive.

"And then he keeps counting the days, checking off with cards or calendars or what else he has.

"It's like any other war that way. If a guy gets careless or does some crazy thing, he's going to get hurt. Okay, so there ain't as many people now who mourn over the ones who die. So call him a victim of circumstances.

"I suppose that's the difference.

"In the Second World War he was called a hero.

"I'm not a draftee. I suppose this kind of war makes it toughest on them, because the big majority of them wanted no part of it, even though a lot of them are good soldiers. I'm no Marine loudmouth, but I think this kind of war is fought better by the guys who have the indoc-trination, the gung-ho training, the specialists. The Army realized that when they put in the Green Berets, trying to build that pride that keeps a man going even if nobody else gives a damn whether he comes out or not.

"I'm not saying that most Americans don't care. I know they do. You don't get thousands of them sending stuff over there if they don't care. And the average Joe over there realizes that bitching in this country isn't aimed at the guy in uniform but at the whole stupid war, and I don't disagree with that language.

"It IS a stupid war. We never should have let ourselves get dragged into it for what passes as a government of South Vietnam.

"But that don't mean that you don't fight, brother, once you're in it.

"And they can call the American a lot of names around the world, but they can't call him a bum fighter.

"Sure, every man who carries a rifle and gets shot at would like to feel that everybody back home understands what he's going through. But if you're a career man, you don't worry about it. You should have known what you were getting into. If you are a draftee, that's the way the numbers go. A man has more things to think about than glory and being remembered."

One who thinks about it and calls himself a dove is Brother Paschal Seifert, a poet and librarian at De La Salle high school, to whom the war is a mockery. In "These Honored Dead" he writes:

> *We have not been burdened with them,*
> *Broken, burned, and gutted men,*
> *Nor shall we bear the memory of them*
> *Who died in swamp and rice field*
> *For a cause they cannot name.*
> *We have seen them die in living color,*
> *Seen them fall between the gum*
> *Commercial and baseball scores,*
> *For we have loved our war games, nicely*
> *Timed before our drinks and dinner.*

Open Wider, the Hygienist Purred

Her long voluptuous fingers moved with easy intimacy among my lower teeth, pausing now when they met resistance from a curled lip and scrunched cheek.

"Try," she said in a confidential tenor, "exposing your incisors."

I sat upright in a posture of instant wariness, modestly raising my clinical bib. There are times when a man's only defenses are his instincts. For several years now dentists — pirating the showmanship of the manicure dens and sauna baths — have been cashing in on man's eagerness to be seduced therapeutically.

The emergence of the busty hygienist is a triumph of the impressario's art in dentistry. The white-smocked cavity plumbers have come a long way in just 25 or 30 years. It used to be a visit to the dentist was equivalent to spending an hour in a boiler mill. Later, it came to be financially likened to the hour before the Stock Market Crash.

Today they have achieved the small miracle of turning a routine tartar job into an erotic experience. The indisputable logic here is that the customer may object to being needled but he doesn't mind being wheedled.

For reasons that need no detailing I resist trips to the dentist, in this case one Richard Trezona, despite his acknowledged skills. Trezona's ancestors settled on the Iron Range and initially made their living wielding jackhammers and pneumatic drills in the iron mines. Their trade lives on proudly in the person of Doc Trezona, the excavating having now moved to Lowry Av. from the jasper drills of Pioneer B. Shaft.

Trezona gulled me down to his office yesterday with the promise of having my gums massaged by a tall, lissome, inner-smouldering hygienist named Midge Shaw, who a few years ago finished runner-up for the profession's coveted Miss Inlay award.

Mrs. Shaw has that surface reserve common to Germanic temptresses. She appeared in the reception office with something in her hand that might have been a carrot but turned out to be a small spear. Her voice was low, with a hint of hoarseness. All she said was, "Come, it's your turn."

It was all the sailors ever heard from Lorelie. They called this one Midge but she looked like Brunhilde. Her face was lovely and her hair was a varied beige that could only be described as smoked enamel. The office radio was on, and I would take an oath the first tune was the Ride of the Valkyries from Wagner.

Her cover story was that she was going to clean my teeth. But she was making surreptitious little marks on some diagram, and I had the lurking sensation I was going to get nicked in some form or other.

She was now into my teeth, nudging suggestively with the little mirror and prying with the hooked explorer. Protectively, I fell back on my athletic training and tried the tongue-and-cheek version of hockey's shell defense. With this, I could give Brunhilde only the upper left hand corner of the back teeth to shoot at, tightening up the angles on the rest.

She now clamped an agreeable but firm Prussian hold on my head and countered with the water syringe. Her quarrying became more insistent, more aggressive and, for one scary moment, vindictive. "Brunhilde," I asked, "are you married." She nodded yes, and asked why I inquired.

"Because you're going after my upper teeth like you had a bad day with the old man. The last thing I need is a vengeful woman working on my molars."

With this, she thawed quickly and crinkled her lips, although the movement was hard to verify as a smile because she was looking at me upside down. In her hands was a length of floss, dropping in a long loop below my chest. I was a sitting duck. "Lady," I said, "I just want to be cleaned, not garroted."

She performed her maneuvers with high professional finesse, however, finishing with a langorous frontal buff job.

At this point Trezona entered briskly, took the mirror and began putting some moves on me with the probe. "I was doing better with Brunhilde," I told Trezona. "I think your technique is good, but it's your Latin chant that bothers me." He seemed puzzled.

"Every time you say something to the hygienist in code," I explained, "it comes out 50 bucks in translation."

He finished with silent gestures, using the semaphore system — one finger for a cavity, two to recommend a bank loan.

Shrinking Bubbles in Milwaukee

The distress signals from Milwaukee's hundreds of beer cellars are beginning to fade, foreshadowing the end of the resistance by a great and gallant people.

The town is about to run out of beer.

For weeks it has been under siege, its taplines systematically drying up in the face of a brewing industry strike. "It's like the Tommies at Tobruk against Rommel," a bartender told me last night from the scene of the encirclement.

"Milwaukee can take it," he said with an ashen but indomitable pride. "We're down to the six-packs and small kegs. Most of the taps have shriveled up and most of the joints only have bottles and cans now. The good Milwaukee beer is almost all gone. It tears at your heart to see your customers, wan and thinner now, trying to stand erect at the bar and not betray the hurt inside them when they order 'One Round of West Bend Lithia.' And then we all cry together, the way they did at Leningrad."

Into this foamless sea of weltschmerz I placed a telephone call last night to a couple of neighborhood bierstubes in the hope of restoring this once gay city's flagging morale. I would have sworn the first dim response was, "This . . . is Milwaukee."

"It's like Atlantis," disclosed Tom Belfer of Murray's Tap on the lower east side. "We're going under in a few days unless the strike ends — bubbles, bottlecaps and all.

"I don't mean all of us will run dry. I drove up to Pewaukee a couple of days ago and bought a load of

Meisterbrau, made in Chicago. They stuck it to me on price, but I swallowed hard and paid it. See, I operate a super-bar, one of those long 60-footers. I'm strictly on volume because I sell at 25 cents a bottle. This is strictly a shot-and-a-beer joint. Nobody messes around with style. They come up and order a Pabst and a Coronet. That's brandy. It may not be sophisticated but it sure as hell is inflammable.

"Now, you can't get Pabst today to save your soul. I've actually seen young women of otherwise spotless character forfeit their single most priceless possession to absolute strangers for one bottle of contraband Pabst."

"And this most priceless single possession," I observed sorrowfully, "is, of course . . ."

"A season ticket to the Packers, what else?"

"The thing is, you have to live in Milwaukee to appreciate what a strike against Schlitz, Pabst, Blatz and Miller's does, not to the economy, but down deep, I mean the soul of the city, the way the guy says with the covered microphone in front of the ruins on Ch. 3. This joint, they come in here in swarms. As a matter of fact as I'm talking to you I'm looking at a couple who been in here since 6 a.m. They're working on their second case of Heileman's and I don't know if they like it, but somehow it don't seem to matter any more."

Civic reputations do not usually overwhelm me. I have seen some routinely strong performances at the rail in Milwaukee, but nothing materially better than at Mayslack's in Minneapolis or the Liberty Bell Snake Pit in Hopkins. And so I called Grain Belt's Bob Grodahl for the trade's verdict of Milwaukee, straight from the vats.

"It's unreal," Grodahl revealed. "The amount of beer they drink in Wisconsin and Milwaukee. The national average is 17 gallons of beer annually for everybody alive in the United States. In Milwaukee it's about 30. In Minneapolis, now, everybody over 21 drinks an average of 35 gallons of beer a year. In Milwaukee it's between 50 and 55. The only thing close in Minnesota is New Ulm, where half the residents are tuba players and have large capacities. What I'm saying is that even if Grain Belt went round the clock, and asked our workers to forego one of their five beer breaks a day, the industry still could not keep Milwaukee supplied in this emergency."

Sobered, I dialed Kastelic's Bar in Milwaukee, where Pabst drinkers reportedly had refused to humble themselves with other beers and were copping out with Jim Beam whiskey.

"That's right," declared Virginia Kastelic. "For the Pabst drinkers in this joint, switching to another beer is like Charles Boyer eating hotdogs. This is a Pabst town. We got one Schlitz drinker here, and nobody talks to him. Two, if you count Jose Ferrar in the commercials.

"Somebody told me there's a brew called Schmidt in the Twin Cities. I tried it but couldn't find them in the telephone book. Here when you say Schmidt everybody in the joint thinks your calling his grandfather."

I communicated this conversation to Belfer of Murray's Tap. "I ain't mentioning names," he said grimly, "but there ARE limits. Nobody drinks swampwater in Murray's. By this I don't mean Schmidt's or Grain Belt. It's a terrible time for Milwaukee, and if we all expire together, they'll have to change the slogan."

"To what?" I asked.

"You have to see it, don't you? The biers made for Milwaukee's famous."

The Ex-Bishop Takes a Bride

All who are smitten by fairytale romance must regret that the lively campaign to canonize James Shannon as a trailblazing bishop has been interrupted and possibly postponed by his recent marriage.

For a while it looked as though Jim was only one letter away from sanctification, if not by the bewildered Pope then at least by the local cassock coalition—which eagerly awaited each new mail pouch from New Mexico for fresh documentation of Jim's several agonies.

In the finest tradition of the Elizabethan sonnets, however, love has surmounted all. Everyone is going to survive in his fashion, the ex-bishop, the Pope and even Jim's earnest follower in the local priesthood who ventured the surprising theory that the bishop got married as a result of mental exhaustion.

This may have impressed the psychiatrist but does absolutely no credit to the bride. Normally, now, the world greets a wedding with festivity and buckets of rice. This one, on the other hand, has occasioned an international weeping binge unmatched in Catholicism since Notre Dame blew the national title in the fourth quarter against USC.

The Pope has expressed his sadness. Archbishop Byrne has expressed his sadness. Bishop Cowley has expressed sadness, along with most of Shannon's lost battalion of padres in the Twin Cities. I can think of no other marriage capable of launching global melancholy on this scale unless it might be Truman Capote's or Hugh Hefner's.

Well, enough. The newlyweds deserve our best wishes

and undoubtedly will live happily ever after in their comfy adobe hacienda near Santa Fe.

Jim, as you recall, wrote the Pope some time ago resigning as bishop because he couldn't teach it the way the encyclical said on birth control. Jim then wrote to the newspaper saying he was resigning. When he got married he wrote the Pope again, but did not overlook the New York Times.

This has put the Pope in the awkward position of not knowing whether to write to Jim, or a letter to the editor in the Times or try for the Saturday religion page in The Minneapolis Star.

While awaiting the couriers, I think we can pretty well deduce the most recent conversation between the papal nuncio and the papal secretary.

"It's from the one in St. Paul," Luigi the secretary said wearily, "the letter-writer. This has got to be the end. We could live with it when he resigned. But now, well, there is no other way to say it, the bishop has gotten himself check-mated—in other words, your excellency, married."

"Have you checked the afternoon mail? I mean there's always a chance he might ask for an annulment."

"No, no. This looks like its for keeps. According to ecclesiastical law, it calls for automatic excommunication. Now I know excommunication doesn't mean what it used to mean in the old days, I mean consignment to the Lutherans and all those things, but it's still a pretty tough rap."

To this the nuncio held up a tranquilizing hand. "There's no need to take any action at all. All you do if you excommunicate the fella is to force him to start writing his letters to Abby Van Buren. At all costs one has to keep his options open. I think the lesson of Bishop Shannon is that we simply have to put down 1969 as a rough year for Irish politicians. Don't we have anybody in Washington who can

talk to him? Who's our man in Washington? No, not the
cardinal the one over the cardinal?"

"Mr. Lombardi, a layman athletic coach."

"Fine, I like the sound of all those syllables. Now don't
we have an equally headstrong Italian in the Twin Cities?"

"Yes, a baseball manager. I saw him on television last
night and when he went to the mound I was scared to
death he was going to deck Perranoski."

"Well, what about enlisting this Perranoski?"

"A LEFT HANDER?"

"Be that as it may," said the nuncio, "there is no call to
regard James Shannon's decision as irretrievable. After all,
he has asked to stay on the reserve roster as a sort of aster-
isked bishop. I admit I never heard of a bishop listed in
the footnotes. But these are extraordinary times. Aside
from resigning and getting married, has he done anything
REALLY objectionable?"

"Like buying season tickets at Gustavus Adolphus? No,
nothing like that. He did get married by a Protestant minister but the guy's name was Hugh Kelly, so we still have
hope of getting that one back, too. I think we can all relax
now because there shouldn't be much more mail."

"Have you ever thought about our mail," asked the
other, "when they have their first quarrel?"

Joe Zilch Makes the Box Score

An hour before, his audacious deed was on the lips of thousands. His reckless base-running left the multitudes awed and his breath left them nearly anesthetized.

For an invincible moment he stood with the mighty, vaulting out of the obscurity of Lawler, Iowa, and the second-deck beer counter for one unforgettable dash to glory. Indomitably he charged into the infield from the third base stands. His gait was furious if uneven, making it a tossup for the startled fans to guess whether he was coming out of the bleachers or the Peanut Bar at Webster's.

He passed third at full lurch, shouting, "Pals, this one is for Carew." Halfway to second he launched himself into a Four Gravity fallaway slide, churning sand and pebbles into a geysering cloud, like a commando hitting the beach.

With a buoyant triumph in his heart, he bounded off the field, waved to his thundering public, and loped into the first base stands. They clasped his hand. In the heady ecstacy of the moment he thought it was Killebrew. It FELT like Killebrew.

What it was was a Bloomington cop, embracing the breathless base runner with an earnest hug and the time-honored greeting: "That'll be 100 bucks, Ty."

This may not have broken a record but it did break his cash reserves, and as a result the galloping Hawkeye became the first athlete in Met Stadium history to hold his post-game press conference in jail.

"How do you like it," he mourned. "I give them the

best play of the afternoon and they want to fine me $100 for stealing second."

I wanted to extend the hand of sympathy but was prevented by the unsympathetic steel bars. Instead, I maintained a cool professional detachment and asked what he thought was the turning point.

"I flew up from Iowa for the weekend, okay. I'm a Twins' fan. So I celebrated Saturday night, and, brother, they don't pour them in Iowa the way they do here. I'm watching the game Sunday with some other guys from Iowa and we're drinking a beer an inning.

"Then somebody says, 'if you got any hair on your chest you'll show us how to slide into second, like you been yellin.' Well, it's the seventh and I already had nine beers, which is a complete ball game you might say, so I just took a direct exit.

"Plus we had a little friendly bet and all I figured to get was thrown out, nothing like 90 days or 100 big ones. So I broke when the vendor finished his stretch. Could Carew make a prettier slide on nine beers?"

"Only Martin," I said solemnly, "could have made a prettier slide on nine beers, and there have been times when he just may have. The trouble is, while you may have captivated the crowd you shot holes in the ordinance. That's a $100 fine. I feel for you. You must be the only aspiring ballplayer who got his tryout at the Met and his release in stir."

But now he emerged from his depression and, with a rakish bravado, announced that he would not meekly submit to the tyranny of Chief Clarence Coster's kangaroo court and might plead innocent to disorderly conduct.

"The prosecution," I objected, "will chop you up. What do you have to match 23,000 witnesses? I figure you can cop out, and the only defense that has a chance is to tell the judge the truth — that your action was criminally inane."

Accordingly, he waited for a buddy to arrive and in due course was bailed out. The buddy identified himself as one Gene Lynn Lynch, a name which has a solid ring but was regrettable, since the guy in the cell already had used it.

"That will be $100 more," said the sergeant, "for obstructing justice." Well, they left on $75 bail, for which Bloomington apparently will now settle. "You should have bailed him out," the officer told me, "and taken him to Fong's Chinese restaurant for a meal."

"Fong would never forgive me," I said. "Whoever heard of a customer sliding into the beef subgum."

"Santa, Do You Believe in Kids?"

Disturbed by a note from a theologian-reader asking, "Is Santa Claus really dead?" I hustled downtown Tuesday to confront one of the old trolls between shifts in a Mall-side department store.

He was sociable but weary with an oddly canted, spavined posture that gave one the impression he was not from the North Pole but on loan from Manpower, Inc., and his last job was carrying hods for Rayco Construction.

"Is Santa Claus really dead, you are trying to find out," he mused. "My friend, I have had the arm put on me, the bite put on me and damp little tots put on me, but this is the first time I have had a stethoscope put on me. You sound like the coroner sent you and what he wants for Christmas is me."

"No, no, you do not understand," I comforted him. "The thrust of that question, as the theologians would phrase it, is very pertinent. The trouble with you people up there is that you are out of touch with the great social upheavals of our time and for 364 days of the year your only contact with the alien world is with a few seals, submarines and the guy from White Bear who goes up there every year in a snowmobile."

The troll's ringleted beard stirred vigorously, momentarily giving him the appearance of one of Dayton's Van Dyked promotion executives after meditation. "I understand you perfectly," he said. "You want to know whether youth's restless stirring for independence, the challenge to authority, the wish to re-fashion institutions; whether all of this has had an effect on that most durable institution of all, Santa Claus."

"I could not have said it better," I observed, impressed, "myself."

"Well as a matter of fact," he continued, "it has. In the end it will be all for the good and certainly a lot of it was overdue, but it does change things. For example, the letters I get from the kids for presents. We used to call them, rather simply, requests from the kiddies."

"And now they are called?" I inquired.

"The kids are now calling them demands. I got one the other day from Richfield and the kid said he wanted a box of Tinker Toys and this was not a request but an ultimatum. Well, of course, you know the kid is going to get the Tinker Toys eventually but I had to consider my image so I said I would hold a dialogue with the elves and then bow to the ultimatum with dignity.

"But that is the spirit of the age, you see," he continued, "and you encounter it from kids of all colors and nationalities. You could try to resist, I suppose, but that is going to get you stamped as an old fogey and eventually get you shoved out of the sleigh, and besides what do you do if a bunch of the little kids decide to pull a sit-in? I don't have that many potty-chairs in the bag to go around.

"One thing you can't argue about. It's true that Santa Claus has come down through the ages as part of the Caucasian establishment, and that is wrong no matter how you view it. I want to change that and, before the TV networks discover the idea, I'd like to turn over the sleigh and reindeer every fifth year to Dick Gregory.

"The whole concept of Santa Claus and the reindeer is too northern-European-oriented, as though Santa Claus is a Norwegian. To account for other cultural heritages, one of the deer ought to be replaced by a lion and another by a pony."

"You want to be careful there," I interrupted. "The first thing that is going to happen if you come down here with lions is that they're going to be auctioned off by the Como Zoo."

"And so Santa Clausing in 1968," he agreed, "is an entirely different position. Closer to home, for instance, I have problems you might not have considered. What it is, you ought to know, is the elves. They are restless themselves and are forming boards and committees. They want things like bigger pensions and more happy-frolicking time and 12-tone toe-bells. And they are coming with petitions and now they want to screen some of those letters. Plus some of them are getting openly critical of my fat appearance and have rather publicly advised me to switch from sugar plums to Sucaryl plums.

"But, I tell you, no matter how much I love them, it's a jolt to realize that some kids just may not believe the way they used to. You got any encouragement?"

Friend, I know you would have told him the same thing. "Yes, Santa," I said affectionately, "there is a Virginia."

Ah, Sunset over the Junkyards

The advertising geniuses and resort promoters who have been trying to coax more vacationers into Minnesota now admit privately they have been overlooking one of the state's most novel scenic attractions.

It took a rank amateur in the travelogue business, State Sen. Norman Larson of Ada, to clear their fuzziness with his ringing tribute to the diversified charms of the automobile junkyards of Minnesota.

We will disregard for the moment the quibbling point that Sen. Larson owns a junkyard harboring a thousand rusting relics.

No, the senator is a crusader in the classic and historic mold, a man of dimension and vision. He wants to save the automobile graveyards of Minnesota, more or less in their natural state and presumably uncluttered by such garish gimmickry as hedge shields, Lombardy poplars and stands of pine trees.

What they do, he advises us with a paternal sense of disclosure, is prevent accidents by breaking up the monotony of rural scenry. They inherit this humanitarian role from billboards, abandoned culverts and Quaker State signs, which used to be our first line of defense against monotony on the prairie.

If you decline to buy this logic, Sen. Larson gives you a second choice. By putting all of the automobiles carcasses in one place, he says, you can simply "close your eyes when you go by."

There might be some embarrassment, admittedly, if the

guy driving from the opposite direction does the same thing. In the case of the senator's own junkpile, we would then have 1,002 rusting wrecks.

But we ought to give serious thought to promoting the hundreds of pristine, largely unspoiled auto cemeteries of Minnesota in line with the senator's suggestion. It's important to remember that any town can show you something unsightly. But it not only takes acreage and imagination, but a special kind of squirreliness—a fondness for stashing things away—to produce the truly breath-taking fendered forests that attract tourists.

While I realize this is just a sampling of the unlimited junkyard vistas open to the tourist, I'd like today to inaugurate a Scenic Tour of the Auto Graveyards of Minnesota, in the hope it might add depth to your understanding of the Minnesota countryside:

Hanging Hubcaps-in-the-Pines, just outside of Hibbing. This is a particularly historic setting, in the heart of the Minnesota Iron Range, giving the tourist an otherworldly feeling as he views the great terraces of mouldering radiators. The reason for this is that most of the iron in the junkyard came from the pits not far away. The tourist may then regard the scene solemnly and muse: "Ah, dust-to-dust. That is the way of it." Recommended for reflective travelers, serious students of the development and trends in American automobile garbage piles. Tour departs from Keewatin. Scenic Highway 169 runs not only by the junkyard but *through* it, imparting greater intimacy to the view.

Monoxide Gardens, between Northfield and Farmington. Here, amidst all that drab, unrelieved monotony of rural Minnesota we find a veritable jewel of contrast, a junkyard bulging out of Highway 3. Special attraction here is a sort of honeysuckle oasis separating ten corroded Chevvies and six overturned Opels. Readily accessible to Twin Cities tourists. Some may regard the chassis motif as a little toney for midwestern tastes, but balance is achieved through the strategic placement of three battered Hudsons among the more sophisticated Buick derelicts.

Rustic Radiators-by-the-Road, a few miles north of Red Wing along Highway 61. Here we have a departure from the normal junkyard design pattern. Most auto graveyards have a sort of casual chaos about them. In this one, the metal may be rotting and unsightly but at least it is neat, row on row in the fashion of a hydraulic petunia garden. For the tourists' benefit, the most picturesque monstrosities are placed near the top of the hill. Picnickers will enjoy lunching by the nearby Cannon River, close enough for sportive travelers to sail a hubcap into the junkyard.

Dodge Dell, north of Jordan, not far from Shakopee. This carburetor glade along Highway 169 is particularly dramatic after a heavy rain, which forms deep ponds among the piles of hulks. The result is to leave some of the cars half-submerged, investing the whole scene with a lily-pad effect. Little paths seem to wind among the wrecks for inquisitive tourists. A bonus for the junkyard buff: the deep vermilion of the rust, creating a striking effect at twilight.

Three Ran for President...

As a political carnival, the presidential campaign of 1968 is less remembered for its fireworks than its sideshows — the heckling young galleryites and the random sounds of thudding nightsticks, echoes of Chicago.

W ITH THE HUMPHREY CAMPAIGN — The reawakened torment of Chicago — with its screaming agitators, cordons of cops and shrill obscenities — is spreading new grief and bewilderment over the campaign of Hubert H. Humphrey.

In a nightmarish half hour in a Seattle arena Saturday, Humphrey saw one of the triumphs of his campaign for the presidency, a singing, foot-stomping rally of nearly 7,000, turned into a flashback to Chicago by 200 antiwar demonstrators in the gallery.

In Seattle, Humphrey was the fervid evangelist who, with the stage prepared for a full-throttle hour of revivalism, was sandbagged before he ever got into the tent.

Despite his thirty years of political warfare, his nimble wit and his legendary reputation for fast talk, Humphrey has not yet been able to cope with he tiny platoons of hecklers who are ruining his meetings and obscuring his taunts of Richard Nixon and his scorn of George Wallace.

He is stunned, standing there in mid-platform, to hear himself called a warmonger, a murderer and even—Saturday night—a racist, to see himself depicted on posters as an American Adolf Hitler.

He tries reason and humor, eloquence and tough talk,

gentle, paternal chiding and hard-eyed ridicule, but none of it works. They stand in the second-deck galleries, singly and in clusters and now in full group, and scream "Stop the war, stop the war!" and then, "Dump the Hump, dump the Hump!"

And Humphrey finally squares about to face them directly, wordlessly, his arms crossed. He is enraged but immensely sad, and he seems to be saying, "Why me? Why me?"

A half hour earlier he had entered the loop-edge arena as the centerpiece of a tumultuous scene of exultant bands and applauding thousands, most of them workmen and their families. It was a politician's Saturday night, a gala for the beaming Democrat who grew up in a tradition of Saturday night bean feeds and rollicking party rallies.

To a presidential candidate whose campaign trail has been overlaid with party chaos, defeatism, setbacks in the polls, small crowds and disunity at the top, it was a throwback to the old-fashioned blowout. There was a fervor in the crowd to match the Kennedy fall of 1960, a never-never land for the politician.

Maybe now, he might be saying, we are ready to roll.

Actor Gene Barry warms up the crowd with a song and a salute to Humphrey. The crowd wants to yell and have fun, and Humphrey senses it and can barely restrain himself to have at the microphone. They start chanting, "We want Humphrey, we want Humphrey."

"And you're going to get him!" shouts Barry. With this he brings on the dialect comedian Bill Dana, whose exact role on the program is not clear, but the mood now changes abruptly.

"Tell some of your Mexican-American jokes, you God-damn racist," one of the protesters yells down to the platform.

"Me, a racist?" Dana asks, incredulous. "Me, a Hungarian-Jew?"

Dana begins fencing with them, asking to hear from a spokesman, but he is gradually losing ground. He wants to let them talk out their aggressions, to bring their abuse down on the platform before Humphrey speaks.

"End the war, end the war," a voice shouts. "Get the hell back to Los Angeles, you racist son of a bitch."

Dana now speaks solemnly. "Hubert Humphrey will end the war for all of us," he begins. "Hubert Horatio Humphrey was supporting the Negro, the Mexican-American, and the worker, before you were ever born."

They jeer him down. He uses all of the standard putdowns of the night club entertainer but they won't work tonight. There is a hatred and vehemence in the small gallery of protesters that needs Humphrey himself as the target.

Humphrey is sitting in a front row chair on the platform, his arms crossed on his chest, his jaw outthrust, more aggrieved than defiant. He wants Dana to sit down, although he understands what the entertainer is attempting to do. Dana has now gone nearly fifteen minutes without appeasing the frenzied protesters, and he stares at them, angry but still theatric, his arms outstretched in a gesture of conciliation that he holds for a full thirty seconds.

The Washington Democratic candidate for governor annoys the hooting exhibitionists a little more with a short talk right out of the handbook of the old politics, using the booming tones and vocal tricks from Sen. Claghorn and the 1920s.

They bring on Sen. Warren Magnuson of Washington, who mercifully keeps his speech short. Humphrey is now introduced and walks to the microphone, smiling, arms waving. He has come to excoriate Nixon, to lay down challenges for a debate and to draw him out on Vietnam.

But the raucous young galleryites do not let him come out of the oratorical gate.

"Stop the war!" they scream. A kid with a long handlebar mustache and elaborately sewn knee patches on his faded denim pants stands and shouts: "Get out of here, you fascist bastard."

They stand, individually or in small groups, young men and women, making the stabbing "V" gesture with their fingers familiar to viewers of the Chicago demonstrations. They gesture with their thumbs down, and some of them gesture obscenely with their fingers raised.

Humphrey turns from the lectern to regard them, seemingly with good humor. He offers them time to speak. A few voice standard antiwar slogans but now a mousey brunette with frozen smile holds up a battery-operated loudspeaker and a bearded youth speaks into a small hand microphone.

"In Vietnam there's a scream that will not end," he begins.

Humphrey supporters in the arena start to shout him down. Humphrey restrains them saying, "One set of bad manners is bad enough. We'll keep quiet. We're going to let this fellow talk. Go ahead."

"In Vietnam there's a wound that does not cease its bleeding . . . We have not come to talk with you, Mr. Humphrey. We have come to arrest you. We charge you with crimes against humanity. Stand before the United Nations and the world and let them try you."

Humphrey, still faintly waggish in the exchange, interrupts to say: "Just be sure there's no police brutality. That's all."

The gallery speaker finally sits down and Humphrey wants to launch his Nixon-needling speech.

"Now ladies and gentlemen, I think you should just as well know there is a determined effort being made by a very small group of well disciplined and highly organized people in this country who have made it their business to interrupt me," he says. "Once there was a danger of a tyranny of the majority. Now we face the danger of the tyranny of an organized minority."

The jeering breaks out anew. Secret Service men rimming the platform and in the protesters' gallery stare at the shouters with anxiety and contempt. Humphrey tries to get the meeting going again.

"I shall not be driven from this platform by a handful of people who believe in nothing," he declares.

And now he puts his hands on his hips and glares at them. He has been conditioned to their words and manner but he is seemingly appalled tonight by their rage and bitterness. Some of them verge on derangement in their shouting, blood vessels distended, eyes glazed.

Humphrey has tried being the kindly professor, the Dutch uncle, the bantering politician. Now he is mad.

"Knock it off, will you please," he says coldly. They do not.

He turns to his audience of party regulars and asks, "What do you want to do with this crowd?"

"Throw them out," some yell.

"That's exactly what they want," Humphrey answers.

But this is what happens eventually, more or less. Scuffling breaks out between a few of the hard core protesters and the police. There is no bloodshed. Some of them are pushed toward the exits. Some stay. Humphrey is now free to talk. He starts in on Nixon. The speech is crisp but mechanical. The candidate cannot forget the spectacle of the last half hour. He returns to it extemporaneously, with a voice quavering and eyes moist in emotion.

The protesters, he says, are driving thousands of voters into the arms of "another candidate who takes no stand." "They have singled me out as the target. I feel honored. They have done this because I spoke for the Negro. I spoke up for the Mexican-American, for the worker, I have stood up for the principles of democracy, and I am not going to see them abused or defiled."

He finishes his talk and they applaud earnestly, but the camaraderie of an hour ago has been deadened.

The heavily guarded candidate returns to his hotel from the back door of the arena.

...But Dick Smiled on Schedule

WITH THE NIXON CAMPAIGN — There is an antiseptic orderliness about the 1968 campaign of Richard M. Nixon, a calm willingness to let Vice-President Hubert H. Humphrey do the kicking as long as Dr. George Gallup keeps the score.

The Republican candidate, relaxed and good-tempered, moves about the landscape as a kind of latter-day political samaritan. It is as though the one-time hip-shooting menace of presidential politics, with his five o'clock TV shadow and jowly grimness, has now been sudsed and groomed, emerging as the amiable and available Mr. Clean of the 1968 campaign.

With the presidential election only a month away, Nixon enjoys a long and perhaps unbeatable lead. His strategy is to keep moving and talking without offending. While Humphrey has to sock it to them, Nixon soothes. While Humphrey fulminates and puffs, Nixon purrs.

Time and defeat have dulled some of the old hostilities

that made Nixon a political demon for millions of voters. Not many people appear to hate Nixon any more, although droves of them still obviously distrust him, not knowing whether he is the new Nixon or the old Nixon or a different Nixon or a more mature Nixon.

His crowds are big and enthusiastic. From the podium he does not say so much as Humphrey, in which he is hardly original. Beyond this, however, his language and manner do not approach Humphrey's fervor. His statements have the flavor and noncommittal tone of press releases from national committee headquarters.

There is a simmering confidence in the Nixon command posts, although there is also an unspoken horror of what could happen if the party relaxes its campaign labor and unless it keeps pouring in manpower, missionary work and money.

Nixon's own style is relaxed, the stuff he says is standard. There is an aura of toniness about his campaign, a smooth rhythm that makes the tempo of Humphrey's campaign seem disjointed and vaguely hysterical.

Even the press corps following Nixon seems to move about in an uncommon attitude of refinement and relative affluence. This was accomplished gracefully in Williamsburg, where the journalistic sleuths were housed in plush, colonial suites of the orcharded Motor House Inn, a lofty contrast to some who had just left Humphrey—with the scruffy downtown hotel where the Democrats had to headquarter a day earlier in Nashville.

Thus while Humphrey has to scurry to make up ground, like a midway hawker drumming up customers, Nixon traverses the country in the cordial fashion of the crown prince cantering toward the palace.

His day in Williamsburg and Norfolk mirrors this campaign demeanor. At 9 a.m. he emerges from one of the historic guest houses in this heartland of the revolution, meticulously restored now by millions of dollars of Rockefeller money.

With his wife at his side, he walks briskly down the path, waving his arms, shaking hands with a cluster of tourists outside the gates.

"My, you've come a long way," he tells a matron from Oklahoma, whose eyes now glisten suitably.

His Secret Service guard keeps the party moving toward the Nixon motorcade, which in three minutes arrives at the entry of the Great Hall of the 300-year-old Wren Building on the campus of William and Mary College.

The hall seats all of one hundred fifty people, not much of a political constituency. But this is a prestige occasion, and Nixon's most knowledgeable followers confide that their man secretly imagines himself an egghead despite all of the unhappy words his compatriots used to lay on the academic scholars years ago.

Besides this, there are some 2,000 people outside the building, listening to his talk about the spirit of America via loudspeaker. Among the onlookers are William and Mary students who have been trying to induce Nixon to talk to them publicly on his Vietnam stand.

Their signs reflect their objections: "Speak up, Dick, It Won't Hurt" and "Nixon Is One What" and a reference to the party's vice-presidential candidate. "Don't Rob Maryland of Its Mediocrity."

Nixon finishes his speech and emerges from the ancient building escorted by a swarm of security men, because the crowd is very close here and the placard-carrying students are lining the sidewalk.

Nixon walks straight ahead, smiling, shaking a few hands, ignoring the signs. The students are orderly. Young Democrats among them have been instructed not to raise their voices or to heckle the candidate. The worst one of the protesters attempts is, "Mr. Nixon, we want to debate with you."

Nixon's entourage sweeps down the street, flooring a woman photographer en route. The candidate pauses gallantly, helps the lady to her feet and stands still so she can snap his picture.

The party returns to the guest house and, aside from a meeting with a coalition of student leaders at noon and a taping session for televised campaign material, Nixon relaxes during the afternoon in deference to his competition —the first game of the World Series.

His motorcade to Norfolk at night leaves on time. Almost invariably it leaves on time. His campaigners call the Nixon organization the most professional in modern political history and there is no reason to doubt them.

Nixon travels with a staff of thirty to forty, including two tour directors to handle hotel reservations and luggage, two political specialists to co-ordinate with local politicians, three press assistants, a sound specialist, his physician and a squad of researchers and secretaries.

During the afternoon his staff has been busy putting statements out that include one in which Nixon suggests the Johnson administration has been standing aside while the Soviets threaten to replace this country as the world's No. 1 sea power—a highly sensitive matter in this citadel of American naval and maritime power.

His crowd at Norfolk overflows the 5,000-seat arena. Nixon revises his schedule to make a brief appearance in the auditorium, where loudspeakers will carry his talk to the overflow. With his wife he enters the arena to the sound of vigorously chanting young people, popping balloons and a platform band.

Nixon is not here to make a speech. The format is part

of this year's campaign experiment by both parties, a question and answer session in which friendly interrogators representing the public asked the candidate to spell out his views on the issue.

The crowd is exuberant, responsive. It is splotched profusely with youth, and on the platform with the candidate is a platoon of pretty girls wearing sweaters bearing the large red letter "N."

Nixon's answers to questions on foreign policy, Vietnam, civil rights and law and order represent his stock campaign speech. On the Soviet-Czech crisis he says President Johnson "missed the boat" by not waging a propaganda offensive in advance of the Russian take-over.

About Vietnam, he says he is not so much interested in stopping the bombing as he is in stopping the war, and that he is not going to be the one to endanger negotiations by telling the Communists what he would do as president.

The session lasts forty-five minutes and for Nixon, reveling in a full-house crowd, it has been a good night's work.

His motorcade returns to Williamsburg and arrives precisely on time.

...And George Filled the Streets With Fury

WITH THE WALLACE CAMPAIGN — The candidate stepped from his limousine into the sunshine of a New Jersey rally platform—stocky, combative, snappy. With a thin smile he broke off a military salute, his own stylized version of the fighter-politician's tribute to his shouting public.

He was flawlessly dressed in a black pinstripe, and he spoke with a controlled pugnacity and taut defiance. He had the appearance of a middle-aged jockey who wants to throw out a board of stewards before it tries to run him off for rough riding and elbowing.

The electioneering arithmetic of the day ahead of him was safely predictable, by his aides, his accompanying press corps and the baiting young antagonists awaiting him.

He would speak three times from Jersey to Cleveland, attract moderate-sized crowds totaling some 15,000, require a maximum security police call-out numbering nearly 1,000 cops, promise to jail the student rebels and the dirty anarchists three times, set off four street scuffles in one town and a small-magnitude riot in another and leave swiftly with the town in turmoil but freshly conscious of George C. Wallace.

It is almost impossible to watch the candidate with any kind of authentic detachment. He disturbs, roils, inflames. Here and there he will puncture a hypocrisy of the times with a shrewd, one-syllable, backporch eloquence that is the essence of his appeal to millions. These are the ones demanding a rollback to the uncomplicated life where there are no Vietnams or blacks in the streets or busing or open occupancy or reformers who, Wallace rails, are taking away the fruits of a good man's work and giving it to the unshaven loafers.

In this most eccentric of all political years, it is an exercise in irrelevance to guess what impact George Wallace will have on the election. The most dependable of the statisticians maintain he will get at least 20 per cent of the vote, perhaps as high as 25 per cent, perhaps higher.

At the political cauldron of America in 1968 he both stirs and sips, drawing from it and churning it. But whether he actually produces an upheaval in the presidential process this year or merely threatens to, he is not likely to go away.

"My God," declared a Hubert Humphrey advocate with

the AFL-CIO's political action organization in Newark, N. J., "the guy is taking away some of our people. They're actually buying him. Look at him demogoguing up there, as though he was John L. Lewis' nephew. With Alabama's record on wages! How do you explain people going for that?

"It would be the same thing if the movie customers of the 1930s voted for James Cagney for president."

He stands before the microphone, jabbing the air with his finger occasionally but managing his gestures, a boxer conserving his moves. Some of the things he says are defamatory and others are frank incitements, but Wallace keeps his wrath disciplined so that they do not seem pathological, and hundreds in the audience will nod and say, "he's right, he's right."

The Wallace campaign is not always that grim. He is preceded by a guitar-picking ensemble and a girl duet singing such magnolia imperishables as "Billy Joe" and "Lonesome Me."

While the battalions of hecklers frequently wind up in clangorous clashes with his supporters and the police, some of them try to make a frolicsome outing of their Wallace-baiting. In the process they fashion some of the best wry humor in American politics.

In Cleveland hundreds of Oberlin College students put on elaborate hippie regalia and split into two sections on either side of the auditorium, one heckling Wallace and the other trying to shout it down in mock defense of the candidate under the banner, "Whippies for Wallace."

Wallace introduced Curtis LeMay, his nuclear-conscious vice-presidential candidate. From the galleries the whippies started a football-style pep yell, "All the way with Curtis LeMay, all the way with Curtis LeMay."

It was all highly campusy and for a while even fun, but

the violent passions it skimmed blew off thirty minutes later and the streets filled with hatred outside the auditorium.

This is the improbable moment of the Wallace campaign —a plaidwork of shouting supporters, screaming detractors sometimes ironic, sometimes obscene and sometimes violent, a swatch of cotton-field comedy, and the slogan-belting centerpiece, George C. Wallace.

His rivals long ago stopped scoffing at him. In the eyes of that part of the American political community that calls itself responsible, he may be a menace but he certainly is no crackpot.

His demogoguery is skilled, calculated, dramatically good. As a platform actor he is the best thing in American politics since Al Smith, a better talker than Richard Nixon and a more efficient campaigner than Humphrey.

His recitation of his own record on the racial issue is generally fraudulent, but he has the sound of a reasonable man to audiences broadly laced with latent bigotry, because very few people are going to admit to themselves that they are bigots or racists. And so when Wallace says, "I never ever reflected on a man because of his race," there are hundreds of people in front of him who are willing to believe it because they say the same things to themselves and believe it.

His hold on his audience is tightened by an adroit political sarcasm that flatters the little guy's private conviction of how it is with big shots and the phony character of the things they do and say.

A reporter who viewed them all on tour has to credit Wallace with the best piece of platformese of the campaign in his account of what happened four years ago when he took the lead in the presidential ballot-counting in Maryland.

"And there was George Wallace with 40 percent of

the vote and the commentators couldn't figure it out," he says. "And then they brought on the governor of the great free state of Maryland to ask him what he thought, and the governor says, 'Friends, it's sad, it's real sad.'

"And you know why it's sad," Wallace continues, taunting the establishment—"because all those political experts never talked to the cab drivers but kept talkin' to the pointed-head ivory tower experts who couldn't park a bicycle straight.

"And so finally on that election night it was botherin' so much that they brought on a man to recapitulate the vote. I don't mean he was just any recapitulater, I mean he was the head recapitulater.

"And when they got through recapitulatin' folks, I was runnin' in second place now 'stead of first.

"So friends, what I'm telling you is that when the pointed-heads decided they gonna recapitulate on you, you better be ready, because they fixin' to do somethin' bad, real bad, friends."

When story-telling time is over, however, Wallace harangues—still under control—and the result often is a post-speech street clash—as in Newark, where a couple of heads were cut open by police clubs, and as in Cleveland, where the abrasiveness of the afternoon erupted in the sounds of kids provoking cops and the splat of clubs on the kids' heads.

He calls Richard Nixon a two-faced hypocrite and Hubert Humphrey a slacker. He does not use those labels, but this is an academic quibble. His audiences understand what he is saying.

He invokes the name of the dead Robert Kennedy his people once reviled. He does this respectfully, solemnly, with voice lowered, as though sharing an intimacy and a devotional with working class people who may not have loved Kennedy themselves six months ago but who now respond to the name ritualistically.

His appeal has the combustible scent of imminent violence, and his manner is a reachback to Huey Long and Father Coughlin. In the name-calling colloquy that erupts between the candidate and his jeering detractors, the language is hopelessly perverted and meaningless.

They call him Hitler and he, observing their bannered swastikas that seek to classify the candidate, calls them Nazis and anarchists.

When it is shorn of its bayou earthiness, what Wallace's rhetoric is really suggesting is one-man government.

"I'm gonna see to it that nobody is ever again gonna make you bus your children where you don't want to have them bused.

"The anarchists better enjoy themselves, because after Nov. 5 they are all through.

"This movement is gainin'. We got newspaper people with us all the way from Paris and Germany. Now, I'm not campaignin' for votes in those countries—yet."

This last purports to be campaign whimsy, but it has a chilly breath to it, a thin insolence meant to make the political orthodoxists squirm.

And when he is through, Wallace leaves to mixed chords of adulation, hatred and the grunt of club-waving police.

This is what happened in Cleveland.

His antagonists in the galleries are loud but mostly orderly, rather easily over-ridden by the extra-decibel power poured into the loud-speaker system by Wallace campaign technicians.

He inveighs against Nixon, "who looks at the open occupancy law and says it's great, when he's in Washington, but he goes down to Miami and tells those southern delegates, 'I'm sorry, real sorry.'

"And Hubert Umphrey. He calls me a Hitler. Well, I fought against Hitler, and I was wounded in combat, but what I want to know is what was Hubert Umphrey doin' during the war?

"I wanna talk about what they doin' to you, those pointed-head bureaucrats and preachers and politicians who don't think the American people know how to act unless they get some guidelines.

"They spend their time writin' reports, and most of those reports come from the big tax-exempt foundations, and you know what they tellin' you? They tellin' you your taxes are gonna have to go up but they sit there and nobody is taxin' them, the muti-million-dollar tax foundations. Well, it's gonna end when I'm elected president.

"Now I'll tell you about Vietnam. We can end that war with conventional weapons. We trying to end it diplomatically and politically, and if we can't end it that way we got to try to end it militarily, and if we can't end it that way, will you kindly tell me what we doin' there in the first place?

"I think any American has got the right to say he doesn't want the war. Senator Kennedy did that. He dissented. But he didn't get up the next morning and say he wants the Communists to win, like some of them do at our campuses in Ohio and California and Alabama. Now there's dissent and there's treason, and raisin' blood and money for the Communists is treason, and after Nov. 5 the ones who try it are gonna end up where they belong—in a cell, in jail.

"They gonna build police academies and all kinds of fancy things like that. But all they got to do is let the police enforce the law that's there now. The way it is, you get your head smashed on a street and the one who does it is out of jail before they get you to the hospital, and the next day they want to jail the cop who arrested the guy who did it."

For 2,000 in the Cleveland Arena, Wallace had the sickness of the country diagnosed cold, right on the money. For a handful of the detached, it was possible to recognize truth in some of what he was saying, and also to recognize cheap, cunning fraud in his snap reading of history—that the people to blame for the race rebellion were the ones who had been beaten down and not their keepers.

His solution to Vietnam appeared to be a threat more than any interpretable policy; his solution to the inequities of big government to strip down the democratic process and replace it with an automatic rifle.

The crowd yells, "Sock it to them, George!" The protesting college kids leave—except two girls, who now walk down from the gallery and into the auditorium aisles carrying a placard urging, "Stop Wallace, Now."

Wallace sees it and hears the rising anger among his supporters.

"Let her have the sign," he says generously, "she has a right to carry the signs."

A big-shouldered man wearing a Wallace straw hat strides toward the girls, gathering speed and rage as he nears them. He swings his fist, ostensibly at the sign. He strikes one of the girls on the jaw. She drops the sign, begins to weep and is led out of the auditorium.

Five minutes later the rally ends and the student demonstrators mill on the sidewalk and in the street. One of them jumps onto the hood of the car that will take Wallace to the airport.

It seems a deliberate provocation, in the fashion of Chicago. The protest needs its martyrs. The police supply them. They pull down the student, bang him in the ribs with their clubs. He squirms and thrashes. A club lands on his head and blood geysers from the wound. He is dazed and semiconscious, lying on the sidewalk. But this is approximately what he sought.

Other protesters, here and there, get involved in shoving matches with police. The police rush them down the sidewalk, goading them with clubs and taking all of the fight out of them.

Wallace supporters stand nose to nose with them on the sidewalk. One says he is a Vietnam veteran and where were you, he asks a student wearing comically patched pants—"You goddam draft-dodging queer!"

They hoot and shove and the police stand watching because no blows have been struck yet, and there might be some sort of ordinance about this. It degenerates into the juvenile insult-flinging of a playground argument, and the police line the streets, arms-length apart, for two blocks.

The bystanders leave, and the police stay at their stations, the new poll-watchers of the American political campaign.

Geritol Beats the Devil

For years he has masqueraded as an ordinary mortal, John D. Peterson — state public servant, Dale Carnegie orator and mountain climber.

I am going to expose this pretense of normalcy today, however, and reveal John D. Peterson as the authentic Indestructible Man, technically listed as 57 years old but faintly immortal.

I made the discovery on a 70-foot perpendicular pitch of Devil's Tower in Wyoming Thursday and view it as a service to Peterson's friends and insurance underwriters to disclose the truth.

A few of you may be familiar with Devil's Tower, a volcanic fluted pillar shooting vertically a thousand feet above the Belle Fourche Valley west of the Black Hills. It is one of a kind, stark and alone among the humpy and forested buttes of the countryside, an architectural remnant of a lost age.

Among the celebrated rock formations of earth, it belongs on the geological midway — a mutant to be observed but not admired.

People who climb look on it as an almost irresistible clinical problem. In so doing they must drop the sham that mountain climbing must be accompanied by some dewy-eyed ardor for the nobility of nature. The Tower has no such nobility; its climbers can have no such pretension.

Peterson does not; nor, if I read my own impulses truthfully, do I. The ideal of mountaineering is to indulge

your need for expression in an environment that can stimulate you physically and spiritually — the grace of the high
country that should be shared by others of the same instincts.

The tower is not this kind of environment. And if you
then ask yourself why climb it, the most merciful response
is that climbing is, after all, an adolescent adventure; and
only this can explain why I picked up the telephone the
other day and called Peterson at the State Department of
Economic Development.

"You want to drive," he repeated slowly, "from Minneapolis to Sundance, Wyo., Wednesday night, a distance
of 650 miles; then get up at 5 a.m., climb the Devil's
Tower with me, and return to Minneapolis Thursday night,
all in a space of 34 hours."

"Why dawdle?" I asked. "You got anything more important to do?"

He is a bald, lanky, energetic man with the persuasive-
ness of a confidence dealer turned legit. Four years ago
he tried to talk me up the tower, but I needed his psychology less than one four-month physical overhaul to shed
the excess 50 pounds that left me bobbling, shamed and
enraged, at the end of the rope on the 70-foot chute.

You have to understand the immensity of a man 57
leading a climb on Devil's Tower. It is comparable to
Murry Warmath entering a Watusi contest or Harold Le-
Vander qualifying for the drag finals at Raceway Park.

Peterson deals with age simply by refusing to acknowledge it. I'm sure he must have taught Satchel Paige how
to pitch in another life. He had already climbed the tower
three times. I insisted he do it again. It was not that the
thing was hovering there, tyrannizing the rebuffed climber.
But there ARE some private disciplines to which one sub-
mits himself, very personal anvils he approaches warily

but deliberately. And so we roped up on a cold, windy morning.

He jammed, chimneyed and frictioned to the top of a broken column. I belayed him from below, but the axiom on the tower is that the leader does not fall. As protection for the front man, the rope has more moral strength than tensile strength. Any drop of more than 10 or 15 feet will yank the pitons and carabiners from the wall in the fashion of a chain of shredded safety pins unfastening in unison.

I joined him a few minutes later. Peterson now attacked the pivotal pitch of the climb, the 70-footer. He would not do this many times more, and I marveled at his drive despite the rising fatigue. All the disclaimers aside, this one was a cruncher, a brutal exercise in high-angle gymnastics.

He got up. I charged after him, literally. This was the holdless impasse four years ago and there was no point in sparring. It went exuberantly fast. I did not argue with the absence of handholds. When the friction ran out, I substituted fervor, which has less substance than granite but a lot more suspense.

The pitch ended, Peterson greeted me with a droll handshake. "Don't tell me you aren't glad to lay the ghost."

I decline to accept this invitation for an eloquent announcement. "Bwanna," I said, "keep going."

We did, to the top. And, of course, the ghost IS laid, isn't it?

"Until the next one," Peterson clucked.

We split a fifth of Geritol and rappelled down.

A Recipe for Red Faces

Before you go any further here today I want you all to congregate in the kitchen, solemnly touch your spatulas to your foreheads and sprinkle ceremonial flour on the kids.

Will you then please clasp your doughy fingers together and, in unison, pledge undying love and loyalty to the rival houses of Pillsbury and General Mills. Say a little limerick for Pillsbury's Doughboy and, to prove your neutrality, give Betty Crocker one vigorous sift.

With these devotionals out of the way, you may then ask how it happened that the recipe for Pillsbury's $25,000 prize-winning marshmallow rolls has been appearing in substance in General Mills' cookbooks since 1963.

To forestall any immediate rioting or potato-masher assaults from Hopkins, let me assure you that absolutely nobody is questioning the originality or artistic genius of Mrs. Edna Holmgren, the grand championship Bakeoff winner, and certainly nobody is questioning her accuracy or zeal with a potato masher.

The facts are these: A few weeks ago Mrs. Holmgren, a civic-minded kitchen virtuoso who is also village clerk of Eden Prairie, won Pillsbury's best-of-bakeoff award with an enthrallingly delicious roll called Magic Marshmallow Crescent Puffs.

Basically, it is a sugar and cinnamon-coated marshmallow wrapped inside Pillsbury's crescent roll refrigerated dough. She had been making them for eight or nine years, first with a complicated yeast dough process that her neighborhood pals never quite mastered.

Some time ago she shifted to the refrigerated dough, cut the process from three hours to 15 or 20 minutes, and won the big bundle at Atlanta. As a result, Pillsbury is now selling great tons of crescent roll dough.

A few days ago I received a letter from a Brooklyn Center housewife — you will allow me the small independence of not using the antiseptic word homemaker — declaring:

"Can you imagine how horrified General Mills must have been when a recipe with slight variation from Betty Crocker's Hostess Cookbook won $25,000 in the bakeoff?"

Having been thus lightly greased, I had no recourse but to get myself thoroughly rolled by calling on the richly battered bureaucracies of General Mills and Pillsbury. Both displayed a lofty, correct professional etiquette.

Still —

I cannot say for certain whether my correspondent from Brooklyn Center is actually a onetime playground chum of the mischievous General Mills public relations operative, Glen Gaff. By a fluke of events, Gaff is in Mexico this week — which may mean either that General Mills had a very good year or Gaff had a bad one.

Anyhow, from the flour bins of General Mills came this announcement from Betty Crocker: "Our buns were called Hocus Pocus Buns at first printing in 1963. They were called Balloon Buns in the Hostess Cookbook and this year's spring recipe brochure . . . The end result is similar to the recipe (Magic Marshmallow) you are referring to.

"The lady who won must be terribly thrilled and excited and I am sure sincere about her entry. She could easily have developed the recipe herself or gotten the idea in a conversation with a neighbor."

General Mills, she explained, got its own recipe from

one of its homemakers of yesterday in its vats along Hwy. 18. Allowing for a couple years' lead time in installing it in the cookbooks, this can only mean some providential bolt of AC-DC current struck the kitchens of both Mrs. Holmgren and Betty Crocker at about the same time.

A few hours ago I received a sealed, hand-delivered communique from Pillsbury, defined by its author as "a position paper on Magic Marshmallow Crescent Puffs."

"The Pillsbury Company," it said in part, "recognizes there is no really 'new' recipe . . . and that in most cases when women create recipes they begin with another recipe and add their own special touches. This year the Pillsbury Bakeoff recipes can be easily classified as new inventions and up-dated traditions . . . The idea of putting a marshmallow inside a crescent roll dough is new. Both the Pillsbury Company and the Bakeoff judges were aware that a similar idea had been published in a less convenient form."

And thus I spent some money to ask a free-lance cook, Betsy Norum who, coincidentally is a former employee of General Mills, to bake batches of each. General Mills, of course, has no refrigerated dough. It took three hours to do the GM rolls, a half hour for the Pillsbury.

Both are delicious. I now have before me one of our advertising men who deals with both companies, and will ask him which roll he prefers.

He is looking at me with profoundly sad, soulful eyes.

"I think," he is saying, "I am going to cry."

War in the Parking Lot

Before the lawyers and physicians get into the scene, I think you should join me in spreading the ointment of good will on the wounded feelings and contusions left by last week's Met parking lot brawl.

You will remember the dark-fated Twins' pitcher, Dave Boswell, struggling into the clubhouse after Wednesday's game with the report that he had been assaulted by some primeval giant weighing 260 pounds.

According to Boswell's biographers, the assailant possessed the dimensions of Samson and the menacing manner of a deranged judo wrestler.

Having been spurned when he offered Boswell a postgame snort, the giant is alleged to have rabbit-punched the defenseless stroller before being routed by an avenging platoon of Twins. When last viewed, according to this version, the well-greased dragon was driving rapidly toward the southern Minnesota cornfields with a half dozen skulking companions.

The first impulse here, naturally, is to rejoice in another triumph for the legions of decency and honor. There is something about Boswell's genius for squirrel-cage drama, however, that suggests another version.

So for those who are intrigued with the anatomy of a brawl, I traced the creature from the stadium's asphalt moors and discovered him to be none other than one Gene Jasinski, an authentic Samson from Faribault and generally classified as the merriest giant in town.

"It just didn't happen the way it was written up in the

papers or the way Boswell said," Jasinski mourned. "All I did was slap him on the back and tell him to keep on winning and it ended up in a riot. I'm almost always a happy man. This is horrible, what happened, I wasn't drunk. Nobody in the party was. I was just trying to be sociable. This neat, paneled bar I own — where Billy Martin himself has quaffed a few — my softball team is afraid to come in now. They tell me they're scared to death I'm going to congratulate them by slapping them on the back."

The problem with Jasinski's pat on the back, you understand, is that it has a seismographic impact that can be compared only with the eruption of Krakatoa. What happens to its recipients is what happened to Pompeii at 79 A.D.

In Faribault he has been institutionalized by pals and golfing confederates as "The Polack," a term which in this case connotes lively fondness and considerable awe. "You know the game you play with kids and put a marble in one of your clenched fists and tell them to guess which one," one of the clan volunteered. "Jasinski plays it with footballs. He would have won the country club driving championship years ago but he's impatient and tries to ambush the ball. As a result, he's usually lying two on the railroad tracks, and where the rest of us play with a caddy, The Polack plays with a surveyor."

Boswell loyalists will understand immediately how there must have been some inevitable zodiac force impelling their man into an encounter with this usually harmless but often aimless missile from the prairie. Sooner or later Boswell gets next to most of the calamities on earth.

The one from Faribault approached him amiably. "I knew he was a ball player," Jasinski tells us, "but I didn't know which one, and I just wanted to say hello and tell him how great we think the Twins are, so I offered him a drink and said 'good going.' Then I slapped him on the back, like you do. And now I might have been a little off and my hand landed on his neck, but I didn't mean anything more than what you would call a good-natured pat."

Earnestly, the Polack sought to demonstrate on me. He telegraphed the move unintentionally, however, and I was able to absorb the main blast with a beer tray grabbed hastily from the bar. Still, I went numb momentarily, and expressed my appreciation of how the misunderstanding could have happened.

"But when he came back and asked for an apology," Jasinski continued, "gee, I felt terrible and said, sure, Dave I'm very sorry, and put out my hand. But do you know I was standing there with my hand out and the guy swings a right at me and uses some bad language, and there's where everything went black."

The first thing that went black was Boswell's eye. "Didn't you turn the other cheek?" I asked. "Hell no," Jasinski said. "If I turned the other cheek I would have knocked the guy cold from the collision."

"The worst part," a Faribault informant said, "is that Martin himself almost got dragged into the middle. He's been a favorite in Faribault long before they found out he was a generalissimo. We made him an honorary deputy sheriff. It's almost too awful to think about. He woulda had to arrest Boswell as his first official act."

Bread and Water for the Groom

Enemies of corruption will be gladdened to learn that one of the last vestiges of the wastrel life in suburbia — the wild stag party — has been shot down by the ferociously vigilant Bloomington police.

The emerging hero of the piece is the indomitable police chief, Clarence Coster. Mr. Coster is rapidly gaining fame among lovers of law and order as the Sir Percival of Penn Av. and among the worried scofflaws, as the Bald Beagle of Bloomington.

Make no mistake about it. Mr. Coster is a good cop, one of the best in the country. He is not only able, tough and savvy but well-spoken, sometimes whimsical and always light-footed, a combination that no lawman since Charlie Chan has achieved.

You may have heard of the smoothly military style in which the chief's forces routed a platoon of revelers a couple of weeks ago at the Howard Johnson Motel not far from the Bloomington-Edina border. As yet unpublished, however, is the lofty spirit of self-sacrifice with which Bloomington's finest knights approached the struggle.

Now there are arguments still before the courts in this, so it is not appropriate to question the innocence of suspects, merely their marbles in risking the amateur status of the party's honored guest, a bridegroom-to-be.

Some of the facts in the case are not in dispute. Pals of the bridegroom organized a bachelor party at the inn to pay suitable respects to the young tycoon's last days as a free and untrammeled spirit.

Toward this end, two young ladies were enlisted as entertainers. It has not yet been determined officially what form this entertainment took, but you can assume they weren't hired to play harps.

News of the impending drama reached the police via one of the community's uninvited and disgruntled rakes. The chief's first move was to infiltrate the party with a double agent especially trained in detecting budding decadence.

"It was much too demanding and hazardous an assignment," Coster explained later, "to ask for volunteers. In addition, our men are so high-minded I doubt that any of them would have volunteered in the first place.

"In the end, I had to conscript a man who, through a process of straw-pulling and coin-throwing turned out to be one Paul Petersen, a very dedicated officer of handsome bearing and tolerant mien."

Officer Petersen duly insinuated himself into the party, paying, the police contend, $12 for the privilege of wishing the bridegroom bon voyage.

Meanwhile, in the corridors and driveways, the brisk but orderly bustling of police officers bespoke the calm pursuit of duty by an aroused constabulary. Officers moved with practiced stealth behind the available concealment — ferns, drapes, large empties of Coca Cola and small sofas.

Indoors, however, in best tradition of the theater, the show went on. Officer Petersen steeled himself by reciting from J. Edgar Hoover, and remained forthright in his attention to duty.

The party grew noisy. Borrowing from the casebook of Inspector Cluseau, Officer Petersen pretended to join the imbibers but, despite some nose and chin gymnastics, merely succeeded in spilling beer down his chest.

Two of the revelers, uncontrollably stimulated by now,

joined the young entertainers. This made not two but four non-harpists, a coeducational quartet. On signal, police emerged from the ferns and strode into the arena.

They were promptly ignored by the revelers until somebody tumbled to the distressing truth. Four people hit the window without the formality of opening it. Rounded up, they were escorted with 28 others into the waiting bus, whose company nameplate had been turned discreetly into the exhaust to avoid embarrassment.

It is with some regret that I recite the toll of the arrestees. The cops netted not only the bridegroom, and the best man, and some of the leading candidate-millionaires in suburbia, but two inquisitive ministers, among them the minister who was to have officiated at the groom's wedding.

It was, truly, an impressive roster. The cops did not escape unscathed themselves, we might add. One of them was lacerated going through the window. And a squad car, hauling some confiscated booze to the station, got hit by a car and had to limp heroically into the garage, seeping Jim Beam on its erratic course to sanctuary."

"Our men," declared Mr. Coster with pride, "came through it in relatively good condition, attesting to their advance level of training."

So far as I know, the wedding is still on, the bride's theory being everybody is entitled to an off-night now and then. And so blooms another fairy tale romance.

———

Incidentally, they all got off at the subsequent trial.

The Town Culture Couldn't Kill

BALTIMORE, MD. — The city of Baltimore, justly renowned as the Mammy Yokum of eastern culture, mounted a civic welcome for the Minnesota Vikings today with a lynching party at the Three Jays Bar.

In a gesture of charity toward our men, the boys at Three Jays used a stuffed manikin. Normally when they hang visiting football players in Baltimore, they do not bother with effigies.

"We're havin' one minute of vigil for the Vikins," explained the man in charge of the wake. "We do it ahead of time for the visitors because if our guys lose we're gonna do it to the Colts.

"Between you and me, I give you guys credit just for comin' to town. The opinion around here is we're gonna chew you up, and the last guy in the world I would want to be Sunday is this quarterback Joe Krab."

I interrupted this monologue long enough to correct the spelling and to feel inside my vest for the comforting little bulge of the pearl-handled derringer I usually carry in Baltimore.

There is no question about it, the town has that familiar glassy-eyed, red-veined momentum for Sunday's NFL Western Conference title game between the Colts and the Vikings, starting at Memorial Stadium here and on CBS at 1 p.m., your time back in the snowdrifts.

The conditions here are mostly dry and boisterous, and undoubtedly will produce a new record reading on the decibel machine Sunday in the world's most deranged stadium.

Baltimore is the place, you may be aware, where Nudnik got his start. By a freak of topography it has by and large escaped the westward spread of art and science from the city-states of Athens and Sparta, and the advance of the English language from London.

It is surrounded by a big league menagerie that includes the social lions of Virginia, the political tigers of Washington and the stock market bears in New York, yet it has happily clung to its own woodland and is still regarded fondly by visitors as a sort of uncultured squirrel of the mid-Atlantic.

"Baltimore," groused a businessman-native at the air terminal, "died culturally a hundred years ago after the Civil War, and each succeeding generation feels it has to sign the certificate all over.

"They can't get excited about the things that excite other towns—the huge building programs, downtown rehabilitation, education. All they get excited about is the Colts, and they better not lose two in a row or they'll run THEM into the ocean.

"About anything else the town is so indifferent even the black militants gave up on setting up some kind of riot last summer because they couldn't get enough people interested.

"What the town is, is a fish market where everybody rests on Sunday to scream his damn lungs off at the football game, and it doesn't matter who they're screaming at. Their idea of culture down here is a game of four-handed bumper pool."

Despite my own reservations about Baltimore I viewed this as a needlessly stern judgment until I stepped off the airplane. I dropped a quarter into the shoeshine machine in the men's room and the machine wouldn't work. I dropped in another quarter and it didn't work again.

I headed for the baggage claim downstairs and was stampeded. By the hundreds they were storming the tiny luggage stalls, unidentified as to airlines or day of the week. It was wild, dangerous and hopeless, an example of what would have happened if the Aqua Jesters remodeled Wold-Chamberlain Airport.

My baggage, I discovered two hours later, was still in Chicago. Shortly before midnight, five hours after I got here, my luggage rejoined me. I am writing you outside a small Chinese laundry. In Baltimore, you make do.

And yet in the midst of all this disorder, the Baltimoreans and their custodians of the press are keying themselves by measured degrees for Sunday's contest. By this morning it still had not reached a convulsive level. The newspapers, for example, were sedately occupying themselves publishing proposed nicknames for the Colt defensive line. "Satan's Four" was suggested. So was "The Eat-A-Quarterback-for-Lunch Bunch."

Gulping at this, I headed into the Three Jays and was instantly spotted as a Minnesotan by my habit of pronouncing words by syllables instead of paragraphs. The argument, although good-natured (they really are a generous group, you know) began immediately on civic affairs.

"Tell me, what have you people done about Urban Renewal?" I asked.

Although temporarily slowed, my antagonist responded boldly. "Well, I ain't heard lately so he must have been put on waivers."

And so the debate raged while the Vikings strode closer to their appointment with fate. Friends, I realize it's a long shot. We are down by 11 points in the odds right now and the locals can barely restrain all the talk about Super Bowls and Lunar Bowls.

But it's demoralizing for a visitor from Hiawathaland to get rebuffed on the simplest people-to-people things here. I ask if they have heard about General Mills and the guy at Three Jays says he should have joined the Navy. I ask about Stanislaw Skrowaczewski and he says what round did we draft him on.

Boys, win one tomorrow, will you? Win it for the Father of Waters if nobody else.

In Sun, Her Hair Was Auburn

Her husband teased her for experiments with her hair, chided her as a natural brunette and an undercover blonde. But when the sunlight touched her hair in mid-morning it evoked a saucy auburn gaiety that seemed in rhythm with her spirit.

It lit the whimsy and the spunk in her and stirred her husband to tell her—in the last three or four weeks when the time had passed for make-believe — "You good and wonderful Irishman, you're too stubborn to die."

He breathed the words again today at Ft. Snelling Cemetery, where English-born Maureen Kemble, thirty-five, was buried.

In another month she would have lived to see him receive the college teaching degree to which she had committed the last five years of her cancer-scarred life.

"I tried to get her to stop working," her husband said, "but she would tell me we were in it together, and even when she knew it was going to be all over for her, she had this idea that a teaching degree for me meant the whole world for her, and the kids after her.

"She had her faults, but until the very end she would laugh at her troubles, and when she was afraid, she would tell only me. God, she was a good woman for me. It isn't a fancy eulogy, but I know she would know what I mean. I never saw anybody with more guts.

"I met her when I was in the Air Force. It wasn't a bad life for me, but it wasn't going anywhere. She talked about education but I was a high school dropout from St. Paul.

My people had been in the service and that's where I was going.

"But five years ago she talked me into trying to become a teacher and I left the service.

"We both worked, not only so I could go to school but so we could own this house we have in Coon Rapids and give our two kids a normal life, even if it meant my commuting every day to St. Cloud State. She wanted it that way, and she wouldn't change her mind, although the disease was breaking down her body."

Five weeks ago the attrition of cancer forced Maureen Kemble to leave her data processing job at the Minneapolis office of the Social Security department.

By then both of her breasts had been removed. She had undergone surgery for a hip tumor, breast cancer, an adrenalectomy and a hysterectomy.

Her friend in the office could not recall a complaint from her, rarely noticed a change in her instinctive buoyant character, her eagerness to surprise them with small gifts or an impulsive aside.

To her husband she would portray herself as an international gadabout who was born in England, married in Winnipeg, Canada, to an American, conceived her first child there, gave birth in England where he was transferred, learned to be an American stenographer in Las Vegas, Nev., where he was transferred again and an American housewife at 10325 Xavis St., Coon Rapids, where they settled.

Charles Kemble, thirty-one, nodded toward the provincial furniture in their suburban rambler home. "No, she didn't have to work, but it wouldn't have been much of a life for us if she didn't. And I think somewhere in the back of her head she was afraid I was going to give up college if she didn't. And for a guy heading into his thirties, with two kids, there wasn't time for any more false starts.

"Plus that, there was her temperament. She liked the neighbors but she wasn't a coffee klatcher. She would have been climbing the walls being tied in. She got satisfaction working in an office, and even more by knowing she might be building something for the kids when she was gone.

"Right now she's a data processing steno or something like—."

Kemble caught himself talking of his wife as though she might be home tonight. He is a levelheaded man, with no artificial reserve or elaborate outward melancholy. He could talk of his wife and maintain control when he recounted the past, but he stopped and lowered his head and wept when he mingled their lives once more in the present.

He had been an airman for several years when they met in Winnipeg. They were married in December 1956, moved to England the following year and then to the United States, where Kemble left the service in 1963 and enrolled at the University of Minnesota on the strength of a high school diploma acquired in the Air Force.

He worked nights, his wife days. He unloaded pop bottles, worked a gas pump and repaired broken-down burglar alarms. His first two quarters at the university were a disaster, but he re-enrolled, earned an Associate of Arts degree, and for two years commuted the seventy miles daily to St. Cloud State in a car pool.

"The family," he said, "was all over the map. Maureen was in the Social Security office, I was running back and forth to St. Cloud and now I'm practice teaching at Excelsior, and the kids (Brent, 11, and Colleen, 8) were at Mississippi elementary."

His wife learned two years ago that her condition was incurable. The breast malignancy had been discovered five years ago, and a breast removed. For three years it appeared arrested. In 1967 she fell alighting from a bus and twisted her leg. Some time later the injury was diagnosed as a hip fracture, and a tumor was discovered.

Her condition began deteriorating, the periods of pain became more frequent.

"I tried to tell my son as best I could," the husband said, "but nobody is God about those things. I tried to forget her mother died of cancer when she was born. Five years ago the doctor gave me to understand it might not be more than a year.

"But both of us knew the last two years. She was good around the house, and still liked to party, but sometimes she would break down and tell me how afraid she was and about the pain.

"Saturday night we had some pizza with her friends from the office. The next day she spilled a glass of water on the bed, and I asked the boy to look after her Monday when I went to St. Cloud.

"She was in the hospital Monday afternoon when I got back. I went to see her but she was all drugged and didn't know what was going on. That is the really cruel and sad thing about her having to go that way, that we couldn't have had one final talk.

"She died Monday night.

"I don't guess anybody outside her close friends and her family knew her.

"But she was such a good woman."

Fleischman in for Mozart

The society lionesses in town have been after me for neglecting the wedding circuit, the bona fide major league of competition.

"All of us," one complained, "are breathless for the news of the two most dazzling events on the May nuptial calendar, the wedding of Allan Holbert, the music critic, and John Mariucci, the rusty blade from Eveleth."

"I wasn't aware it was a contest," I replied. "What is it you want to know? How they came out? The truth is I was forced to default on my invitations to both and, while this causes me regret, I may have to put it down as providential. I might have drowned at Holbert's wedding and gone up in flames at Mariucci's."

By a stroke of coincidence, however, one of my most trusted agents witnessed both ceremonies and has returned in an attitude of pale astonishment.

"The wedding of your newspaper pal, Holbert," he said, "richly lived up to its billing as one of the matrimonial dramas of the season, the Superbowl of high society. As you know, Holbert exchanged vows with the gracious Jill Irvine of the renowned Irvine and Ordway families of suburban St. Paul. Symbolically, the newlyweds launched their great adventure by paddling across the lake in a rowboat. They could have used a motor, but who wants to start married life by shearing a pin?"

"But I tell you it was a Peter Pan idyll, a lovely fantasy in the wildwood, truly a midsummer night's dream. Unfortunately, it poured. Nothing serious, you understand, but it did make the footing uncertain.

"Many of the hundreds of gaily clad guests were under a canopy near the bar, leaning forward expectantly so as not to miss any of the Guthrie Theater readings. Only a few of the guests fell into the garden. Allen and Jill were superb, inching toward the judge, correcting for slippage as they proceeded, the bride resourcefully deploying her parasol as a makeshift rudder.

"The actor, Robert Pastene of the Guthrie was in splendid voice delivering his Shakespearean reading and I tell you, it was as if on cue: When Pastene came to a passage that went something like 'now a gentle calm is descending from the firmament,' why, the sky shook with thunder and I thought Holbert was going to take the river.

"You had to forgive him, under these unusual circumstances, for a small lapse in his part of the ceremony. I mean he forgot to kiss the bride. But he recovered beautifully and two sweethearts now embraced gently and undyingly, and the skies seemed to take on a roseate shimmer. It may not have been an omen but it was a helluva lot better than getting hit by lightning.

"After suitable socializing, the sweethearts boarded a 14-foot rowboat and set out poetically on Pine Tree Lake —a picturesque pond of shallow depth that required the groom to pole around like Mark Twain here and there but he brought it off without a wrinkle in his composure, although you couldn't say the same for his Edwardian suit. Once there, I would have sworn I heard your pal mutter, 'One of us is gonna have to bail, lady, and it ain't gonna be me,' but the words were a little distorted by the creaking of the oars.

"Cal Griffith, a friend of the family, was there. As Allan and Jill waded into their limousine from the boat on the far side, Cal observed idly, 'It would have been a terrible thing if the rain came before the fifth inning.'

"But now Mariucci's wedding to the former Gretchen Weidman, while it lacked Shakespeare and Mozart, compensated with generous passages of Fleischman's.

"Mariucci, you'll agree, is one of the great democratic figures in our society. Almost everybody got invited, and as the evening progressed they sent out a flying squad to bring in a few off Lyndale. It was a house marriage. The next day the rubbish man counted forty-four empties of Bourbon and Scotch and twenty-two empties of champagne. 'What was it,' he asked Mariucci, 'a party or a raid?' When Mariucci explained, the rubbish man stalked off in a sulk because he wasn't invited.

"Oh, there were a couple of minor fist fights, but a wonderful forty-eight hours for all that. You will be delighted to learn that Mariucci was the image of sobriety much of the time, not touching a drop until 10 o'clock; 10 AT NIGHT, brother, to answer your question.

"Anyhow, few of the guests went home at night so Mariucci wound up on the couch with Bill Leach. He awoke in mid-morning to the scent of smoke. One of the guests trying to burn paper in the fireplace missed the mark and lit the drapes. Mariucci struggled to his feet uncertainly, saw the flames and croaked, 'Good Lord, eight hours after the nuptial vows and it's Dante's Inferno already.' "

The bill will come to two grand. It could have been worse. They could have lit the Fleischman's.

To the Moon Via Family Plan

Stirred by the government's prediction that public vacations to the moon will be possible in 20 years, a Minneapolis travel agency comes forward today with the industry's first package plan to the Sea of Tranquility.

"We have priced it at $19,870," declared William Gregory of Traveling, "under a unique open-end arrangement, which means special allowances are made if the tourists burn up in reentry."

You may have noticed the dispatch a few days ago telling of the forecast by Harold Hornby of NASA, who informed tourist officials in all seriousness that within 20 years they can tell their customers literally to take a flying jump at the moon.

As early as 15 years from now, he said, orbiting sightseeing tours of the earth will be available to vacationers at $2,500 a person for a week, just slightly more than a comparable period at the Minnesota State Fair. Before 1990 you will be able to land on the moon at $20,000 per person for the two-week excursion from Cape Kennedy direct to the lunar lodges, where national park stickers may be required.

"The idea is simply overwhelming," Gregory conceded, "and so I put my tour guide researchers to work on a plan that is within easy reach of most economy-minded vacationers. For practical reasons, the payment must be made in advance.

"You can see the problem immediately. Here on earth if a reluctant customer doesn't pay his balance after the tour we have collection agencies that can track him down. If the space cruiser develops mechanical trouble, on the other hand, the customer will be somewhere betwen Orion and Ursa Major at billing time. We have no collection agencies with that kind of speed, although some have the zeal."

This interstellar brochure, therefore, is being offered to those who have not firmed up their 1990 vacation schedule and may want to skip their annual visit that year to the exciting Radioactive Rapids near Monticello:

Tuesday — Leave the Twin Cities' auxiliary airport at Thief River Falls — the Ham Lake site still being under consideration — via Northwest Supersonic jet at 7:06 a.m. Arrive at 10:45 a.m. in Florida, leaving to a coin flip between the pilot and passengers the decision on what runway to aim for. Change to non-stop Rocket Flight 523, where complimentary champagne tablets will be served on-board.

Tuesday, on board — Rocket departs pad at 12:20 p.m. with the traditional playing of the recorded aloha to space travelers — Walter Cronkite calling, "Go, baby, go." In-flight activities begin with kinescoped movies intended to put travelers in a suitably festive mood, starting with H. G. Welles' "War of the Worlds." Rocket's band plays timely rendition of "Nearer My God to Thee."

Wednesday — Earth-gazing much of the day, the guides pointing out such memorable sights as the great North American Pollution Pall, an irridescently scenic cloud cover spreading from the Gulf of Mexico to the northeast Minneapolis smokestacks. Sports-minded travelers can tune in on the Twins' telecast, to watch Billy Martin raising hell with the grandsons of Twins' farm official George Brophy. Or they may sit in on the spaceball game closer to home. For outdoor lovers, a special nature walk among the asteroids can be arranged via mini-rocket. Revelers experience the rare joys of dancing upside down, the weightless Watusi.

Thursday — Transfer from space station to lunar module. After 2½ days of leisurely travel during which tourists happily master the techniques required by the interspace burp bags, rocketship arrives at the Sea of Tranquility. Housekeeping cabins, some in need of dusting, are available. Lunch in the old-moon atmosphere of McDonalds-by-the-Mare. Those preferring solitude can choose their own crater.

Monday — Golf at the championship Lunar Country Club, where the first fairway measures 3½ miles, the length of the lunar eight-iron. Shutterbugs must exercise some degree of caution in posing their friends. The procedure is not to ask them to back up too far. It doesn't do any good to get them focused if they fall off the edge.

Tuesday — Resident moon combo, The Sons of Buck Rogers, entertain at the showpiece "Dance Under the Planets." For current-affairs lovers, special editions of the Minneapolis newspapers are delivered, unfortunately with the wrong sublunar school lunch menus.

"There's one thing travelers may watch for on the lunar surface," Gregory noted. "Out there past the Sea of Crisis, I'll be damned if there isn't one of Naegele's billboards announcing '243,812 miles to Wall Drug'."

Allison Calms a Dispute

Let us all join in marveling today at the calm logic of Dave Boswell's explanation for Minnesota's finest hour of violence since the Sioux Uprising of 1862.

"I'm a little high strung," acknowledged the Twins wounded pitcher from his convalescence bay in Baltimore.

By way of confirming this reasonable diagnosis, the Red Cross has provided us with fresh statistics from Detroit verifying at least three knockdowns, one knockout, between twenty and twenty-five stitches spread over two of the combatants, five contusions, a suspension, a four-game losing streak and one astonished bartender.

There is no telling what might have happened, people, if Bos had shown signs of temper.

Boswell, indignant with the pitching coaches over slurs on his conditioning habits, encountered Mssrs. Martin and Allison in the Lindell Bar in Detroit, a quiet little riot nook already secure in the sporting Hall of Fame as the former playpen of Alex Karras.

Strong words, as the playwrights would tell it, ensued. Bos agreed to be placated by the club's resident conciliator, Allison. As a token of gratitude, Bos then decked Allison with a right to the chops. Anxious that the disagreement should end there, Bos began kicking field goals with the horizontal outfielder.

This both surprised and disappointed Allison, who now found himself in the embarrassing position of Ralph Bunche trying to mediate a dispute in Borneo and winding up in the community stew pot.

In addition, the mediator's ribs were getting systematically crunched. At this critical moment when the delicate negotiations between Boswell and Allison seemed threatened, the head conciliator himself, Martin, intervened through the swinging door.

There is dispute as to which made the first gesture in the spirit of amity and good will. If it was Boswell, Martin just plain misunderstood. As a reconcilor, Bos had youth and fervor. Martin had faster hands, longer injunctions, four paragraphs in Ring Magazine and gashouse charisma.

With a judicial directness that would have aroused the envy of the great compromisers—Sumner Welles, Dag Hammarsjkold and Tugboat Annie—Martin straightened out Bos with a bolo to the gut, a right to the head, caromed him off the wall with a hook and stood gallantly aside to let him fall into a conciliatory coma.

So much for the essential order of battle. You do not have to take the Ford Hospital attache's word that it was an honest-to-God, black-and-blue, groin-and-knuckle brawl. I have this report straight from the startled bartender:

"Brother, I have seen defensive tackles square off against linebackers. I have seen wrestlers battling stevedores. But I never saw anything like Martin trying to relieve that right-handed pitcher. If they went another round you would have had to get Boswell's earned run average out of the coroner's files."

We are indebted to the Swiss legation for the report that Boswell is heading back toward the Twin Cities from his Baltimore home, in the fashion of the cruiser San Francisco coming back from Savo Island. This is to say he is low in the water and can thank the Lord that his stern is still there because the rest of him is pretty badly shot out.

"As you know," we were informed by the base medical

officer in town today, "the fight happened last week. We held out the news, pending notification of next of kin."

Calvin's first impulse was to ask Boswell to extend his convalescence for another three or four years. His next was to ask Boswell to return to the cities incognito, wearing short sideburns so he would not be recognized as a professional athlete.

Later, Griffith got the second ward report on Boswell and told him: "Come as you are. The dispatcher will think you are a bruised watermelon and keep you in a special crate."

With admirable professionalism, Martin and Allison have expressed the desire to let bygones be bygones. "The thing about Bos," one of the Twins' traveling psychologists related, "is he is a sensitive young man. Oh, I know he almost set off a brawl in the bus by playing with guns, and he had a fight in the parking lot with a fan, and he throws tantrums.

"But down deep he has endearing qualities—such as a helluva fastball."

Whatever Calvin's decision, I just know it won't be influenced by the condition of the thumb on Boswell's throwing hand. This is going to be a flat-out administrative decision, based on club disciplinary policies and maybe just a little bit on how Oakland is doing against the Orioles.

In any event, the league is already nicknaming the mound at Met Stadium Hamburger Hill. If Bos sticks, though, and Martin comes to take him out, I would suggest no argument and certainly no right cross.

Otherwise, Bos, we are going to have the only clubhouse where you get a plasma instead of a shower.

A Bad Season for Disasters

I am going to ask your sympathy and tolerance today in behalf of Radio Station WCCO, the organization which once was privy to the intimate weather secrets of the universe but which now is battling a melancholy slump.

WCCO's dilemma is two-horned. First, it has spent thousands of dollars on new electronic gadgetry and in hiring one of the nation's few private weather prophets with the object of closing down schools faster and declaring roads more impassable than ever before.

Sadly, it has drawn a blank so far this year on storms. The situation has built a towering frustration among the executives and announcers of this worthy station, which fully imagines itself as a sort of climatological Paul Revere of the Upper Midwest.

This, in turn, produces a domino effect of frustrations around the territory. Without storms, the school principals can't call in to get their names on the air. The American Automobile Club, one of the station's subsidiaries which functions as a Triple A farm team in the development of alarmist-type announcers, is frustrated because it is losing air time. Small, unknown two-man businesses which used to get free publicity by announcing they were shutting down at 5 p.m.—usually their regular closing time—join in the suffering.

Secondly, the station's batting average under its new personalized weather forecasting is simply not up to WCCO standard, even in this winter's relatively tame environment.

I don't want to be harsh with the station private oracle, Seth Kemble, an extremely likable, Ozarkian-style gentleman. Seth needs only a few more weeks, I would guess, before he hits stride and delivers us some honest-to-God weather.

You probably are aware that in some respect WCCO is competing with the U.S. Weather Bureau, which on the basis of its buckshot performance of the past clearly could stand some competition.

Right now, in this first year since the two split into separate leagues, WCCO is running well behind and in the forecasters language would be classified as partially obscured. What the station does, of course, is to make use of the Weather Bureau's standard forecasting data and radar reports, and then interpret them to pinpoint weather forecasts and conditions in areas where its sponsors sell products.

This is totally legitimate enterprise, but my friend Seth has faltered now and then in competition with the Weather Bureau, which does not have as much money as WCCO but does have more men. In addition it enjoys the home field advantage against Kemble.

As a result, the most authoritative weather show on WCCO is Maynard Speece reading the Farmer's Almanac at 6 in the morning. This also is a refinement, because Speece used to get his forecasts by examining Roger Erickson's kneecaps.

I monitor the two driving to work in the morning and find them immensely diverting and occasionally legal. My quandary is that I cannot tell whether Speece has a hangover or is simply getting an early start.

And so because of my affection and sincere regard for this radio station, I telephoned my personal consultant at the Weather Bureau, meteorologist Joe Strub, and asked what could be done for WCCO.

"There is nothing wrong with WCCO," Strub said helpfully, "that a good blizzard wouldn't cure. They are in a slump now, true, and at times they actually have not been in the ball park, but they are one of the great heavy-hitters in radio, and they surely will be heard from this winter."

"Are there others in the territory," I asked Strub, "who could use a good blizzard?"

"Well, this is not my field, but I did read a report in your paper last year quoting a University of Minnesota professor to the effect that snow-shoveling, done in moderation, tended to stimulate people sexually."

"And your observation is—?"

"Some of the people I see on the street do seem a little lethargic and sallow. One is thus driven to conclude that there are times when a little snowstorm is what the doctor probably would order."

She Wore a Bikini and Brass Knuckles

For those who have maintained for years that most beauty contests are judged by the blind, crooked or genetically deviated, we have confirmation today from one of the more spectacular victims of boardwalk intrigue.

"When the chips are really down in the big contests," confided Yvonne Bremseth, "anything goes from sex to influence-peddling to fraud. Do you think there's gouging and throat-cutting in a political campaign or pro football game? At Norfolk, a couple of years ago somebody stole my swimsuit an hour before the pageant and another queen, in her most regal and charming manner, tried to burn my clothes off."

The image of all these lovely princesses throwing rabbit punches and psychological grenades at each other before the band starts playing captivates me completely, and more or less renews my faith in the basic competitive qualities of the corn-fed American girl.

I think we should be proud that the young ladies aren't really the unspleened manikins we see on television, reciting the Gettysburg Address and playing the glockenspiel with great feeling and soul. We need a certain amount of malice and skullduggery to make any contest respectable, and I know many girls in the audience will find it reassuring that beauty and brains aren't everything, that conniving still counts for something.

Miss Bremseth functions dually as a secretary with the local huckstering firm of Knox Reeves and as an actress with Dudley Riggs' Brave New Workshop where, by a fluke of coincidence she is cast in the role of a dimwit beauty contestant in the forthcoming "Eighth Annual Unauthorized Son of Miss America Contest," undoubtedly an immortal epic in its field.

There is no other way to say it, ladies, Miss Bremseth is a 10-count knockout, a 21-year-old Okie who, as one of the boys at Knox Reeves puts it, "could play in my dust bowl anytime." Unaccountably, she is working on a four-year losing streak in which she lost out in the 1964 Oklahoma Miss Teen-Age America contest, the Miss El Reno Pageant; was vanquished in the finals of the El Reno contest the next year and lost in the national finals of the Miss U.S. Pageant in 1966.

"Maybe," I suggested, "you should switch to Mum."

"Without being a sorehead," Miss Bremseth said evenly, "because I did win a few, I should tell you that these contests are not exactly all lace and lilacs. At the big time level, for instance, you have professionals who are practically beauty contest gypsies, collecting hair-driers and other merchandise by the gross in prizes and peddling it for cash. There's even a way you can convert a college scholarship into cash.

"You'll find contestants who make a science out of judging the judges. They get acquainted with the contest franchise-holder and put together lists of what the judges like and don't like. Not all judges are corrupt, of course, but most of them are, well, perceptive. A friend of mine entered the Miss Hawaii Navy Football contest in 1958 and got edged out by the admiral's daughter.

"We had an extremely resourceful girl who registered at the hotel for one contest with her daddy, and it was later discovered that the daddy owned the contest franchise, and he was really better described as the girl's *sugar* daddy, and the two terms just don't mean quite the same thing.

"I'm sure the contests in Minnesota are absolutely above board, but some of the local contests around the country are pretty casually-run. I was out-pointed once by a girl wearing falsies and another time by a ballet dancer who was three-months pregnant."

"You have been playing," I commiserated, "in tough luck, Miss Bremseth."

"Well, no, it's just that I need some kind of tactical training. A contestant, for example, ought to watch out for the attractive middle-aged woman judge who very often will vote exactly opposite the male judges because she doesn't want to see all the men drooling over one girl.

"On the national level you have to watch some of the girls themselves, the worldly ones. One of them ducked my bathing suit behind my hotel radiator once. And just before we went on another quarter-finalist came over to wish me luck, bent down to kiss me playfully, left a red lipstick smudge on the shoulder of my white formal and as a parting gesture let her cigarette dangle so that it burned a two-inch hole in my formal's midriff."

Lads, you should have heard what happened in the semis.

Hog Heaven—the Pronto Pup Line

Fondly he fingered a mile-long hotdog, in the style of an afficionado, an antique collector.

"A good item to start on," he said.

Awed, I stood at a respectful distance, conscious of being in the presence of the man acclaimed by the great majority of fry cooks, dishwashers and ham-hock salesmen around town as the most relentless eater in Minneapolis. Mutual friends had introduced us.

"My name," he said candidly, "is Denny Brady, 23-year-old drummer with the Titans, a musical organization now playing at Duff's night club downtown. My avocation is eating. They tell me you have a challenge out to find out whether there is anybody in town who can eat his way through the Minnesota State Fair in an hour and a half."

"That is correct," I acknowledged. "They said it can't be done. I have come prepared with an open checkbook and a green plastic bag into which we may throw wrappers and bottle caps. What do you have in the way of equipment?"

"Talent," he said, "and a set of salt-and-pepper shakers.

"Also, I have been in training the past seven hours and virtually have starved myself."

You should understand that Denny Brady is no cheese champion, being one of the rare trenchermen in the Midwest who eats enchiladas for brunch.

"Right now," he disclosed, "I weigh two hundred eighty pounds, a gain of about forty since I weighed the last time. I do a little trimming now and then, but there's no way of getting around it, I just get a helluva kick out of eating. "The thing is there are so many good things around. Now I don't necessarily care for exotic things, such as meat loaf and salad. I prefer the basic things, but if you think it's all that important, I'm willing to experiment. That little bottle says catsup. Will you kindly pass it?"

And thus we were launched. Denny is a Duluthian, where he grew up on gooseberries and bear meat. He is good company, a sport and an excellent drummer.

His first was the mile-long hot dog with relish and onions. Effortlessly we switched to a bag of Tom Thumb doughnuts as we strode toward the midway, stopping then in front of the bratwurst stand near the grandstand, where Denny acquired a bratwurst with sauerkraut, relish and coke.

"I don't believe in eating aimlessly or anything like that," he said, "but when you go to a fair you just naturally munch. I take off a lot of those calories playing the drums. Some things you have to avoid. That black walnut taffey, now. It's pretty rich."

We plucked a bag of Fisher's salted in the shell peanuts from a concession stand and moved through the midway, where Denny playfully switched to a stick of cotton candy as a change of pace.

"You'll notice," he said, "there's a stand over there saying all the milk you can drink for 10 cents. Why overdo? I like milk just like the next guy, but there is such a thing as style, right?"

Tolerantly, Denny marked time with a box of popcorn while I blew a dollar bill trying to knock out the red spots from a playing card at the shooting gallery.

"It's okay," he said, "take as long as you want. Tell me one thing. Don't you ever get hungry out here?"

"Den," I said, "I get all of my alloted calories with one

Pronto Pup. You have got faster powers of assimilation."

The lecture was lost on my friend, because Brady was already standing in front of the frozen carbonated drink stand, a new concoction of frozen Seven-Up. This he flavored with a small plate of pizza, switching ten minutes later to a moderate plate of tacoes with a side order of corn on the cob, potato salad, pancackes and a cup of orange.

"I have to be back soon," he said, "how about a little dessert?"

"Don't you feel the least bit uncomfortable?" I asked.

"Not really. I usually have three or four ham sandwiches before our first set at the club and all of that gets pretty starchy. This cooler of ice cream now should just about top us off, but there's one thing we've been overlooking that really tempts me — that submarine sandwich in the food service building. They give you Italian salami or cold cuts, or cheese, or cooked salami or lettuce and pepper."

"You can't have ALL of those, I insisted.

"No, just the salami. Now that will be it. According to my figures that comes to about 4,000 calories and $8 for an hour and a half, and if you got any other ideas tell the short order man at the club. I admit I'm full, temporarily. It's been a fine evening."

Appalled, I left the premises but, in a burst of curiosity, telephoned the joint at 10 p.m. to find out whether Brady was in the hospital.

"Hospital, my foot," the floorman said. "He's over at Cascade 9 between sets. I understand he just ordered prime ribs au jus."

Where the Mountains Lift the Sky

For the impatient tourist on a timetable the Grand Tetons are not the country to travel—the soaring temples of rock and ice filling the Western sky above the sagebrush plain of Jackson Hole in Wyoming.

To the north in Yellowstone the Patton-style mechanized charge through the geysers and between the bears may be permissible. It may be unavoidable.

But the Grand Tetons resist breakneck sprints by the hot-rodding hoboes of tourism, feverish package planners with four more waterfalls and a sunset to make today before changing brochures.

Mountain country is the currency of Western travel.

These are very special mountains, grand and impetuous, vaulting restlessly from the piedmont lakes of the valley floor in one sudden architectural sweep that numbs the onlooker on first vision.

In tone with the weather that alters their character, they may ennoble you or humble you or scare you. In sunlight the mottled grey gneiss and schist rock of their highest summits invests the sky with a lyrical radiance, comforting and intimate.

But within the hour they may drain the gaiety from the sky and fill their canyons with storm clouds that very quickly transform the idyll, and the mountains are now fearsome and portentous, the loveliness replaced by a capricious power and hostility.

I view these mountains and the Grand Teton National Park with the self-indulgence of one who long ago accepted that everybody is entitled to nourish a few passions without apology or any elaborate rationale.

The Tetons are mine. I go there every year, by the same routes, with the same appetites. It may be a renewal, a fulfillment, a sense of self-approval for having whipped the dragons one more year, a need to recharge emotionally and esthetically.

On the other hand, it may simply be the mountains, the strength of their poetry—and their ready generosity with a foothold when the climber swears to God that he is about to go over the edge.

Because of these private commitments I know you will pardon me for asking you to visit this place if it is within your curiosity and motive power. I do not urge you to do so.

I insist on it.

Do not go as a souvenir shack gypsy, hastily grabbing instant marvels from the roadside shelves. The supermarkets of American tourism can be found in Yellowstone and in the other tourist stampedes where only the most nimble and resourceful can escape the corrals.

The Teton park itself is stormed by three million visitors a year. But a 10-minute boat ride across Jenny Lake, a half-hour hike, a five-minute drive through the lupine meadows to the start of the Glacier Lake trail will put you into the groves of Douglas fir and Engleman spruce—and from there the mountains.

You do not have to be a climber, a backpacker, a fisherman or a mule to do it. A simple walk will get you there, past the misty froth of a Hidden Falls and now up a few hundred feet to a 7,200 foot overlook called Inspiration point. There—at sunset—you may watch the shadowed summits engulf the saged valley where thousands of sweaty motorists below are wondering where in the hell is all of the repose of the mountains.

In other words, this is country where you do not want simply to sit and be consumed by the scenery. Even caviar gets boring. There is a limit to how far any ogler can be uplifted, transfixed or otherwise dumbfounded, a point of diminishing returns on photography from the highway turnoffs or from the clothesline of the family camper.

You can enjoy the trails from horseback or at a slow-paced stroll. You do not have to rise very high in the forests to experience the luxury of mercifully pure, fresh and aromatic mountain air—the pines, the lingering sage, mountain flowers; or the sounds of the impulsive rivulets bounding from the glaciers.

And a mile above you, lifting transcendent beyond the snowfields and the firs and moraines, are the mountains— the Grand, Teewinot, Owen, Moran, Symmetry.

Now it is tough to assimilate all of this in a day and a half. I suggest closer to five years.

Since this may be impractical, a week or ten days may do. With family, the Tetons are accessible in a leisurely three-day drive from the Twin Cities. I suggest the interstate route through South Dakota, with an overnight rest in the Black Hills, then to the Big Horn Mountains of Central Wyoming or the remarkable Beartooth Pass out of Red Lodge, Mont., or both, en route to Yellowstone.

A five-hour drive through the thermal pyrotechnics of Yellowstone will put you at the gate of the Tetons. If you are with camper, wherever you go, get there early. The park has four or five large campsites, most of them invariably full by 8 a.m. in midsummer.

If you are cottaging or moteling, there is a vast complex on Colter Bay of Jackson Lake, cabins at Signal Mountain further south, accommodations for four thousand in the commercialized but fun cowboy town of Jackson, Wyo.

If the old man had a good year at the office, you may prefer the swank Jackson Lake Lodge or the high-bullion American-plan Jenny Lake Lodge in the center of park activity.

Above all, you have to wander and do things. Look up the Snake River raft trip operators, the rangers who will guide you on breakfast trail rides, and nature excursions. Take the family to Jack Dornan's chuck wagon along the Snake River at the south entrance to the park. Dornan is a rawhide homesteader who regards John Wayne as frilly. He came out West broke forty years ago and now owns the million dollar spread with the Snake River in his backyard and the Tetons just beyond the veranda.

And if the older kids just happen to ask about climbing —thirteen years is not too young—drive past Glen Exum's guide service and climbing school at Jenny Lake. Exum's guides can show them, for $10 in one afternoon, the rudiments of climbing and rope management.

And if they happen to show up on the Grand a few days later, safely and under supervision, envy them. Here is a high-angled ridgeline the climber has just gained, emerging from the shadows into an explosion of early morning sunlight. He may not be able to restrain a small, introspective yodel.

In the mountains here it is hardly irreverent, because he may be a little closer to God, at that.

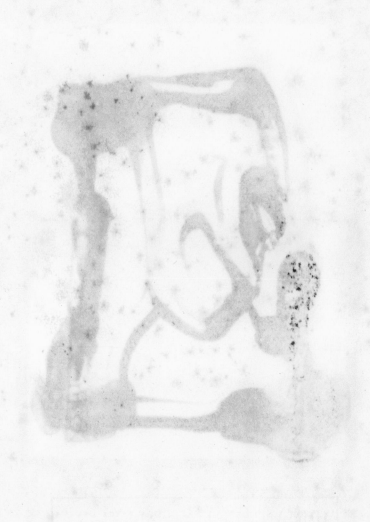

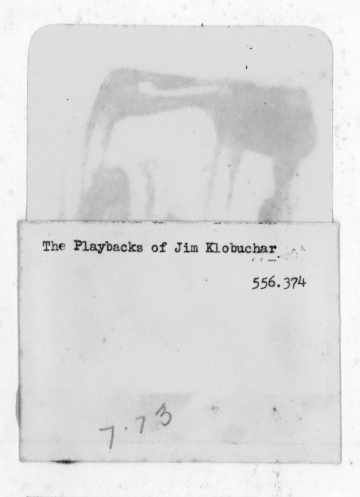

The Playbacks of Jim Klobuchar

556.374

7·7³